Acknowledgments

Wow! How did this book go from concept to completion? Ah, yes, there was that team of remarkably talented and able-bodied buddies armed with cameras, tools, paint cans, homes, goodwill, and so much more who tirelessly came to the trenches day after day.

Doug Smith, you are the most amazing photographer and a dearly loved friend, not to mention one heck of a dancer. This book is a beauty because of you. Sally and Emily Smith, you two win the best in sharing award.

Tom and Kris Lemmerman, you two always go the distance. Not only did you offer up your own home for a junk makeover, but you played a large part, with the help of your crafty crew, in putting Humpty Dumpty back together again in every room in this book.

Judy and "Jer Bear" Cooper, you've been supporters from day one sharing your home, kindness, support, and friendship. The constant supply of tasty treats and wine at day's end was just icing on the cake.

Miss Erica "2NMZ" Sanders-Foege, editor extraordinaire, you offered up smiles, laughter, witty remarks, and a gifted guiding hand. A new friendship was forged that will last a lifetime.

Julie Hanus, you are a person of many talents. It seems that no matter what you were asked to do, you always found a way to get 'er done with a smile on your face and spares to share.

Dougie "blue eyes" Knoll, you wonderful welder, you. You never roll your eyes (even though you may want to) and you pull things off with little to no notice. You are a special friend.

Our families, the Coopers, Coopers, Lemmermans, Haskins, Brookmans, Renards, Musgjerds, and Skartvedts were absolutely fabulous. You rolled out the red carpets and warmly welcomed us into your homes and willingly allowed us to junk them up.

Hirshfield's generously supplied all of the Benjamin Moore and Devine paint products we used in the makeovers.

Many local vendors and store owners provided great junking experiences for us that produced the wonderful junk product for our projects.

As always, our agent Susan Ginsburg from Writer's House helped make this all possible.

To all our friends, thank you from the bottom of our hearts.

Hugs,
Sue and Ki

P.S. On a very personal note, I wish to thank my kids, Elizabeth and Alexander. I'm a mom with a big job and you two have allowed me to do my thing, oftentimes at your own expense. Together you are my center; please always take that with you. Love, Mom/Sue

CONTENTS

REUSE, REPURPOSE, REFRESH   2

A SUNNY FORECAST   4

SHIPSHAPE SUPPER CLUB   22

DELECTABLE DINING   46

LAUNDRY LOUNGE   62

MAKING AN ENTRANCE   78

LIVING ROOM LUXURY   94

A SUITE BEDROOM   116

EXECUTIVE HOME OFFICE   142

SPA AMONG THE CEDARS   160

HOW TO MAKE THE REST   184

RESOURCES   202

INDEX   203

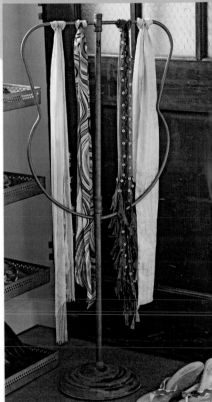

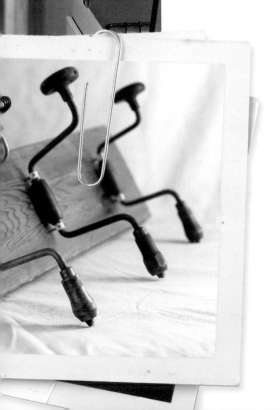

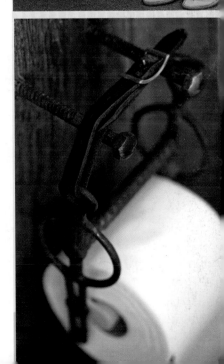

Reuse, Repurpose, Refresh

Welcome to the pages of *Junk Beautiful*. If you find yourself reading this page, either you are already a devoted junker or you are about to become one. Sorry, junking is highly contagious and there's no avoiding it! Our advice is just sit back and give in to the urge.

What is junk? you ask. Some call it garbage, trash, or castoffs. To this we say, "Rubbish!" For us, fleamarket finds, tag-sale goodies, and dumpster discoveries all play an important role in uncharacteristically good home design.

In *Junk Beautiful* we demonstrate how to take the stuff no one else wants and with it breath new life into the decor of your home. People looking for an alternative to their hum-drum, cookie-cutter rooms will find dozens of fresh ideas for showcasing their own personal style á la junk.

After all, it's about time you discovered that junk is for everyone. We show you nine unique styles—and rooms—provide step-by-step projects for the do-it yourselfers, offer up junking tips, and highlight junk transformations through hundreds of beautiful and inspiring photos.

We recognize that like junk, people have personalities of their own; individual characteristics that make them unique. When we are invited into a home to work our magic, we pay lots of attention to the way our clients live. We like to think of it as "meeting the Fokkers." So in *Junk Beautiful*, you'll also get to

know the hopes and dreams of our homeowners.

Junkers are not only stylish people, but they are also concerned about their environment. For years we have been encouraging people to create their own style, one piece of junk at a time. Remember, while doing this we're also saving the earth, one piece of junk at a time.

Until next time, see you on the junk pile!

Sue and Ki

A SUNNY FORECAST

The sunporch was a mess, and all the Coopers wanted was the sun. So we gave them the sun—plus we brought a cleaned-up eclectic style to the reclaimed living space. But let's face it, sunny is a tall order, so we created a room that would deliver a warm glow whether it was sunny or not. The daybed fashioned from a ratty-tatty garden gate anchors the lounging locale—wish number one. Designed with a crafty combination of vintage and inexpensive textiles, the cushion and pillows offer a soft landing pad for weary bones.

Our next task was to provide soothing ambiance. As masters of the mix, we concocted a host of accessory pieces that play well with the daybed,

such as "old meets new" picture frames.

Beautiful and oh so bouncing grand-babies should have their own special wall of fame. We purchased some inexpensive ready-made frames that complemented the decor of the sunporch and slipped in sepia-toned images of the grandchildren. What makes them stand out is how they are hung. The frames are attached with vintage hinges, then suspended from fabulous old drapery tiebacks. A little mix 'n match, now that's cool.

THE FAMILY PHOTO DEBATE

The running debate of where and how to hang photos of loved ones is still alive and well. We suggest you choose an off-the-beaten-path room and hang in group-ings to maintain family détente. For us, the sunporch was an obvious choice but we were lacking wall space—an all-too-common dilemma. The narrow wall that was available was just right for a vertical arrangement.

BELOW The sunporch was too closed off from the rest of the house and had no escape route to the outdoors. A peekaboo interior window and an exterior door and staircase solved the problem.

4 WISHES

Place to Rest & Relax

Designer's Desk

Caffeination Station

Tiny Tot Storage

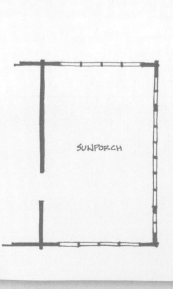

BEFORE

SUNPORCH

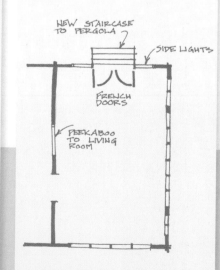

AFTER

NEW STAIRCASE TO PERGOLA

SIDE LIGHTS

FRENCH DOORS

PEEKABOO TO LIVING ROOM

Do as I say, not as I do. Writing on walls is reserved for adult enjoyment.

←— Style Tweak

Are you all over this project, but feeling blue because the style is not speaking to alterna-hip you? Here's a remedy for the contemporary-minded smart set. Paint the frames black, connect with silver hinges, and hang from castors.

Place to Rest & Relax

Prior to diving into a room makeover project ask yourself one question. How will I get the most use out of this space? If you do this, success is certain. The Coopers had big ideas for this tiny area, so it was time to roll up our sleeves. We broke the space into four categories and determined how much space each required. At the end of the day we managed to fit more furniture on the porch, but miraculously it felt more open and functional.

BEHOLD THE BEAUTY OF SUNSHINE

You can't get natural light in every room, so don't squander it when you have a porch. If you have the luxury of privacy, forgo the window coverings in a room of wall-to-wall sunlight. Instead, frame in and upholster transoms above each window for a finished look.

Leaving the windows uncovered will not only shed light on the situation, but also help to create an illusion of more space in a tight room. Sleight of hand is a nifty decorating trick.

"Simple yet stunning" is our mantra regarding repurposed projects. The Lucite handbag-turned-floral container delivers "wow" factor in the desktop design.

LEFT Check out the funky floor lamp behind the daybed. A plant holder wired for light with a mid-century lampshade—it makes quite a conversation piece.

RIGHT A piece of architectural salvage with a mirror added to the center nicely dresses a naked window.

JUNKFO: Architectural remnants are like handbags. You can never have too many. While shopping keep your eyes peeled for out-of-the-ordinary salvaged pieces like the one beautifying the sunporch window.

Lucite bags can be spendy, so look for those with flaws and watch the price drop. Our own bag had a little bubble on the bottom—you'd never guess— probably due to overheating. Who knows, maybe its original owner got caught up in the intense heat of retail therapy! We addressed the handbag's hiccup by gluing on little round feet (wooden drawer pulls to be exact). Now all you have to do is add floral foam and flowers. It's stunningly simple.

ABOVE This room had reason but was lacking rhyme. Well-versed junk furniture and accessories came to the rescue.

RIGHT A garden floral arrangement packaged in a purse offers a refreshing outdoor feel to a sunporch.

1

2

JUNKER'S JUJU

3

We're not intimidated by color. We eat it up. Our muse for this traditional-but-sassy color story was the vintage floral fabric covering the daybed cushion—rich olive and vibrant bittersweet.

1. PAINTS
A. Ceiling, Devine Filbert
B. Wall, Devine Crunch
C. Trim, Devine Olive
The harlequin pattern on the floor was the result of combining the colors to tint stain. Feel free to experiment until you get the color you like.

2. FABRICS
The vintage floral daybed fabric was supplemented by a collage of cloth with rich texture and color. Check the scrap pile at your local wholesale fabric store for the best prices.

3. STUFF
We put together a team of junk that had an air of sophistication for this upscale room—nothing too rusty—small junk items like hinges, drawer pulls, and violin parts.

HOW TO:
Artful nesting tables

Turn the tables on framed botanical prints. Instead of wall art, they can easily become tables without diminishing their value.

MATERIALS NEEDED
- 8 old table legs
- 2 well-worn frames (same shape; different sizes)
- Artwork (we used botanical prints)
- Wooden dowels
- Stain
- Tite Chairs® wood expander

TOOLS NEEDED
- Junker's Toolbox (see page 185)

METHOD
1. Cut 4 of the table legs to desired height and cut the remaining 4 approximately 3 in. shorter.
2. Measure frames to determine dimension of both tables, leaving an inch on both sides and between the top and bottom frames.
3. To attach legs, cut 8 pieces of the dowel to size.
4. Drill holes in table legs to accommodate dowel pieces.
5. Insert dowels into holes and secure with Tite Chair, a liquid wood expander Ⓐ.
6. Finish raw ends of legs with matching stain Ⓑ.
7. Insert artwork into frames and set atop dowels.

Designer's
Desk

JUNKFO: Granny's attic can be frightening, but it's where you can scare up some cool cast-offs, such as an old dressing table. Wave your junk wand and make it a desk. (Feel free to wear a cape.)

ABOVE We removed the desk's drawers because with the glass top, you couldn't get inside them. Easy enough to do, looks great, and the benefit is leftovers for future endeavors.

LEFT Do you have anything lying around your home currently out of commission? We found these lamp bases and put them back to work.

The desk area is just feet from the comfort zone, so no traffic headaches for Judy on her way to work. Lucky girl! We thought this design darling needed a workspace that embraced her quietly graceful style. An outdated dressing table with a few minor alterations is now a fully functional desk. The end result is a workspace that fits Judy as well as those glass slippers fit Cinderella. The new peekaboo window dolled up with garden fencing lends airiness to a tight space.

DRESSED TO THE NINES

Now that you have a foundation, it's playtime. Dress up your desk with things you need corralled in junk containers. Set your inner junker free and look at small junk objects in a whole new way. Seriously, have you ever seen the neck of a violin as a picture holder? The possibilities are indeed, endless.

A desk without a view might be more conducive to getting work done but not nearly as pleasant. In order to connect the sunporch to the rest of the home, we opened the wall and enhanced the new opening with a remnant from a metal gate.

DESK SET

Alrighty then, junk buddies, we're moving onward to the remainder of the desk decor. Wrapped up nicely here is the essence of what draws us to junk. Recycling is first and foremost. Saving a

BEFORE

KODAK E100VS

44 45

ABOVE **Remove, restore, and rethink.** We applied these "re" rules when converting this piece from a vanity to a desk.

trash can from the landfill is a fine example and certainly one for our "junkmoirs."

Once you've come to terms with that, we can move on to the fun stuff. What's the fun stuff? Evoking fond memories, rescuing things from the "no hope" pile, and, last but not least, allowing yourself a quirky grin or even a belly laugh as old junk finds new life. For instance, soda fountain finds will make you feel happy-go-lucky and put the whistle back in your work.

A MIXED BAG OF JUNK

Going eclectic works well for our work-station. While designing, we address both form and function and this curious collection of oddities fits the bill nicely. We adore incorporating different colors, textures, and materials giving shape to a blueprint that defies conventional think-ing. Soda fountain stuff, scrap from vio-lins, concrete salvage, and even trash cans are all viable applicants for desk jobs.

Eclectic does not mean cluttered, par-ticularly on a work surface. Don't fall into the trap of overjunking. To avoid this common problem be selective. Gather your favorite pieces, making sure they all have a function. If you find something new down the road, replace, don't add.

TOP LEFT We spend a lot of time talking trash, but with this projects' trash-can lampshade, we really put our money where our mouth is.

LEFT Bring back the fond memories of the corner soda fountain and your poodle skirt. But beware, it may distract you from your work.

TOP RIGHT Looking for junk that will add a timeless atmo-sphere to your home? Architectural salvage is on our list of all-time favorites. Cast iron rosettes work well as bookends.

ABOVE Don't get high strung, we didn't dismantle valu-able violins to con-struct photo holders. We found a box of scrap pieces at a flea market for less than a song.

Caffeination Station

Make it p.186

TOP Waste is not a part of our vocabulary. The leftover base from the birdcage (now lamp) serves up tempting treats.

LEFT Open the door to a new way of thinking. Just about anything can become a light fixture; yes, even a deserted birdcage.

RIGHT Tying up a napkin with a leftover drawer pull is way more fun than taking the ho-hum standard approach of using ribbons or rings.

Birds of a feather flock together to create this picturesque breakfast nook. The base of the table is a perfectly worn birdbath plucked from the garden. It supports a ready-made glass top. Remember to secure the glass with surface protectors; brunch is always better in your tummy than on it. As for the pendant light fixture, well, let's just say the bird flew the coop leaving its cage for our repurpose.

JUNKFO: When you look at junk, forget what it was and think about what it could be. In this case, our drawer pull became a napkin holder.

Tiny Tot Storage

Make it p.187

ABOVE The kiddie wagon wheels lost their wagon, rendering them useless. Not so fast! Put on a piece of wood and these wheels are rolling again.

LEFT Vintage brackets tend to have beautiful detail and timeless appeal. If you can't find a set, look for singles of similar size and pair them up.

Storage is public enemy numero uno in most homes. There's never enough of it! Laundry rooms and kid spaces can be difficult, but this sunporch presented an even more challenging dilemma: no closets, very little space, and enough toys to fill a half-ton pickup. Like we say, "when the going gets tough, running away is always an option." (Kidding!) Instead, we gladly accepted the challenge and went straight to work. Our charge—among other things—was to stow toys within the porch while keeping said toys out of sight, all while beautifying the space.

We have to admit this undertaking gave us pause, but the answer hit us like a sack of potatoes.

KEEP TOYS IN TOW

For easy access plus storage with a twist, we used convenient covered baskets. To keep the baskets in tow, we designed a very handy shelving unit. We attached lengths of recycled wood to the wall, secured a mishmash of iron brackets to the wood, and placed potato crates on the brackets. The baskets slip in and out making it a cinch for the kids to get at their toys and maybe even put them away! This may sound too good to be true, but one can always hope.

Style Tweak ⟶

Urbanize this shelving unit by switching out the ornate brackets for sleeker ones. Instead of wicker baskets, go for the discarded milk crates that can be found in abundance at a local antique or junk store.

SHIPSHAPE SUPPER CLUB

THE HASKINS

TWO SUPER-
CUTIE GIRLS
ONE DOG
(OLIVE)
RAISED RANCH,
CIRCA 1984

The kitchen is the irrefutable command center of your home. Your heart may not always be there but, without fail, the action is. The flurry begins each morning with that first cup of coffee and inevitably concludes long after most have gone to bed with some-one (who shall remain nameless) sneaking in for a late night piece of pie. No worries, pastry hound, your secret is safe with us!

Our task was to create a family friendly kitchen—functional, yet homey, and thor-oughly modern with country roots.

Our gang was in need of a place to cook, dine, play, organize, share infor-mation, and have a place for Olive, the other dog, to sleep. We delivered every-thing including some nifty reformed ice cream stools.

5 WISHES

A Cook's Corner
Ample Seating
Arts 'N Crafts Table
Mudroom Maximus
Finished Hallway

Let us introduce you to the left side of the new and improved kitchen. It's a lean, mean storing, organizing, and cleaning machine. Everything has its place and every place has a purpose. Kids have their glory, so we say let them shine.

Like, if there must be such a thing as fridge magnets, then give them some panache. Dishes are beautiful in their own right, so why hide them? In fact, why not enhance their natural beauty by displaying them front and center? As for including the kitchen sink, we certainly apologize, but after much deliberation we found no way to avoid it.

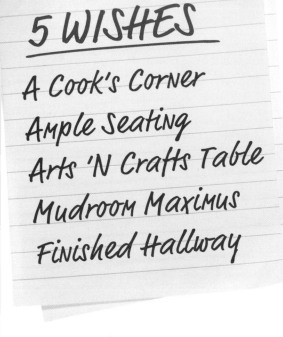

FACING PAGE, LEFT
Old letters and a vintage key hook (mounted on a refurbished cabinet panel) make for a nifty towel holder.

FACING PAGE, RIGHT
Take a bite out of dinnerware storage like some small creature did here, leaving a bit of character behind for our lucky homeowners.

LEFT The mainstay of any message board is, of course, the magnet. You can recruit sundry odds and ends to do the job.

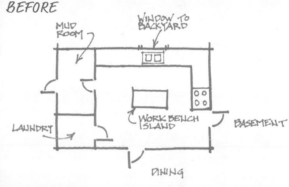

BEFORE

MUD ROOM
WINDOW TO BACKYARD
WORK BENCH ISLAND
BASEMENT
LAUNDRY
DINING

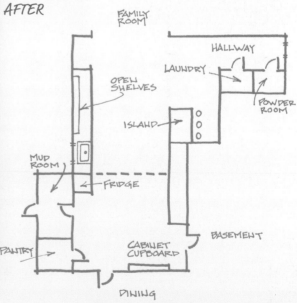

AFTER

FAMILY ROOM
HALLWAY
OPEN SHELVES
LAUNDRY
ISLAND
POWDER ROOM
MUD ROOM
FRIDGE
BASEMENT
PANTRY
CABINET CUPBOARD
DINING

A Cook's
Corner

Fondue night

mommy's way cool !

KODAK E100VS

ABOVE The cats who live here are too cool for this old kitchen.

Should you or should you not remodel with junk? Once you get a taste of this chef's special, you're sure to give the nod to junk. Take a close look at a few great ideas we've cooked up for you. This large stovetop seemed a little undernourished to us, so we rolled up our sleeves, put on our aprons, and went straight to work. The large expanse of galvanized metal needed to be broken up and made more functional. The problem was easily solved by garnishing with some uncommonly good junk.

HOME FOR THE HOLLANDAISE

Every short-order cook needs their tricks-of-the-trade close at hand. Our solution, a chicken feeder plucked straight from the farm. The prep work was a snap, we just cleaned it and installed it. The hood needed a finishing touch, so we wrapped it with slate reclaimed from a one-room schoolhouse.

ABOVE My, oh my. When we spotted this chicken feeder we knew it was the remedy for our contain-it woes. We cleaned it up a bit, attached it to the wall, and BAM! It created perfect storage for cooking essentials.

FACING PAGE Recipes and messages can be displayed and erased with ease on our slate cooktop hood. Looking for something to do while the sauce simmers? Try a game of hangman on for size.

HOW TO:
A clean sweep window covering

A grouping of freshly trimmed whisk brooms, mounted on vintage molding, dresses the window without obstructing the sweeping vista of the great outdoors.

MATERIALS NEEDED
- Architectural molding
- Whisk brooms
- Broom clips
- Skidmore's Wood Finish

TOOLS NEEDED
- Junker's Toolbox (see page 185)

METHOD
1. Measure window opening and cut molding to size Ⓐ.
2. Measure and space whisk brooms according to the size of your molding.
3. Clean and brighten wood with Skidmore's Wood Finish.
4. Predrill holes for broom clips Ⓑ.
5. Attach broom clips with screws Ⓒ.
6. Clip dirty ends off of the whisk brooms and push handles into the clips.
7. Attach window covering directly to window trim.

Junk accessory pieces are not alone in the melting pot of style. The same technique can be successfully employed in establishing the roots of a look. We started with new but vintage, looking cabinets and sleek granite countertops for modern-day utility, all atop a beautiful wood floor harvested from a defunct Sear's store. To cozy it up, we threw in a yummy wicker table as a sideboard and some corner soda fountain ice cream stools (screwed right to the floor for authenticity). A galvanized mop bucket adds fun. Ahh, the look and feel of real junk!

GOING ECLECTIC

"Mingle and mate" is a design approach meant to enrich a home's sensibility, not to clutter or confuse. Our goal here was to do just that, to update without losing charm.

By the way, be discerning while out and about junking. As nicely as a good grouping of junk can work, it can just as easily go south. Many people hurry up and buy to fill a space. When it comes to junk, sometimes you might just have to hurry up and wait in order to find the right piece. Look at it this way, you're making a delightful experience last longer.

Click your heels three times and repeat after me.

JUNKER'S JUJU

Here's a pocket-size junker's manual for a killer country kitchen. Follow these tips and you're sure to take home the blue ribbon from the county fair.

1. PAINTS

The main course served up on the kitchen walls is Benjamin Moore®, Asian Jute. The ceiling sides are Hirshfield's ceiling white and Devine Almond. With your coffee, pair Devine Steamer in the mudroom and hallway.

2. FABRICS

We were fortunate enough to find vintage fabrics in vibrant reds and whites to complement the decor. If you can't, do some research and find reproduction textiles that will spice up your design menu.

3. STUFF

A medley of junk items were used in this kitchen makeover. Among our favorites were casters, both old and new.

Ample Seating

LEFT Hidden under the glass hood of the food server is a vintage steering wheel set on a lazy Susan base, providing the get up and spin for our veggie roundabout.

FACING PAGE, TOP LEFT When it comes to wine, we don't play games. Discarded game pieces glued to cork make a fabulous coaster.

FACING PAGE, TOP RIGHT This easel is constructed from piano parts and castors. As for the vintage sign, a mom can always dream.

FACING PAGE, BOTTOM Veggie slicers sold on TV have made this sweet one obsolete. Don't say good-bye, re-purpose it!

Make it p. 188

Bear in mind, some things are so stunning that whether or not they actually work is completely beside the point. Case in point is our big "happy hour" timepiece, which always reads ten 'til six. The other good news is that it is always dinnertime. Ah, the beauty of make-believe.

The host of our dinner party is a lazy Susan fashioned from a vintage steering wheel connected to a timeworn piece of wood. The honored guests include Mr. and Mrs. wine coaster, one a bottle capper and the other made from game pieces; our cheese and cracker crony, an old vegetable slicer; and best friend, a sign easel built with piano parts.

Like many, the Haskin's were craving an informal space to dine, entertain, and just hang out enjoying some good old-fashioned family fun. In order to accommodate this wish, something had to give. In this case, it was an exterior wall. The back wall of the kitchen was knocked out, providing the needed floor space. Now it was time to get down to the nitty-gritty. A long island was added not too far from the cooking area. Behind the island we left plenty of room for the sideboard to keep the fare close at hand. Just for kicks, we brought in unconventional seating.

When dinner is over and the dishes are done, this counter can act as a family fun center. A good game of Chutes and Ladders® anyone? Also, as the two little ladies grow, it will make a great home-

All this and they can build, too. Life is good!

JUNKFO: Don't let traditional design rules hold you back when lighting a room. Blending is better than matching. A great mate for a bare bulb fixture just may be that crystal piece you've had your eye on.

Sweet Details

Here are some junk accessories cooked to your liking.

1. **TAKING A SPIN** means something different when you redesign a steering wheel into a classic lazy Susan.

2. **LET THE SUN SHINE IN!** Beautifully filtered light can be achieved by simply adorning your window with a vintage wooden screen.

3. **CLEAN UP WITH A SMILE** An old croquet mallet holds down the fort as a playful paper towel dispenser.

4. **MAKE LEARNING FUN** by transforming math game pieces into whimsical and eductional refrigerator magnets.

5. **GLASS** is always good. An unused urine specimen bottle employed as a pencil holder is proof positive.

6. **CELEBRATE** your child's creativity by prominently displaying his or her artwork in a reclaimed metalicious window frame.

work station under the watchful eyes of dear old Mom and Dad.

CONNECT THE DOTS

We've established that the dining nook wears several different hats in this kitchen. Location and accessibility of this multifunctional center were pivotal when plotting the new quarters. We needed to plan the dots and then figure out how to connect them. The counter is attached to the cooktop. It's across from the sink, within sight of the family room, and right around the corner from the laundry room. Wow, looks like Mom and Dad will have a good view of those darling daughters no matter what their task.

Arts 'N Crafts Table

FACING PAGE The old kitchen island is revamped to store hardworking wares and creative kid stuff. Add a bottom shelf, a milk bottle carrier, and some cool red castors and call it a done deal.

LEFT Yes, it's a recycled specimen jar. But no need to get queasy. We buy "old" new stock all the time. That means the piece was purchased but never used, or so they say. Seems a little more like what the doctor ordered now doesn't it?

A kitchen is half-baked without a family command center. The workbench that held center stage in the old kitchen was far too fetching to dump. With a few extra ingredients, it was transformed from island to a post for work and play. Now it sits happily just to the right of the stove so Mom can keep an eye on her brood while she sautés string beans.

FUNNY JUNK

Junk accessories should always be functional, but often we search out items that possess a certain sense of humor. It was a good day when we came across a stockpile of specimen jars. Believe us, they can hold a whole lot more than urine. Pencils are just a start. Go crazy, throw in some rubber bands and paper clips for a perfect desk trio. If you're a more daring junker, try them on for size as juice glasses.

What comes out doesn't always go back in. Maybe a crowbar will do the trick.

Style Tweak

We wanted to add a touch of industrial flavor to our kitchen, hence the galvanized downspout flower vase. If cottage cute is more your style, employ a can of white spray paint posthaste.

Slapstick junk is only one way to lighten the mood in a room. A little clever thinking and a willingness to push the boundaries will also bring some whimsical relief to a classic space. We couldn't help but smile when we came across these downspouts at our local salvage yard.

PASS THE PICKLE

Like sides at a restaurant, accessories in a home shouldn't cost a bundle. So for two bucks each we didn't hesitate to pick up these gutter pieces. When we presented them to our homeowners, the looks on their faces told us they understood. Flowers in downspouts? But, of course, my dear!

COMBO MAMBO

Combinations play an important part in developing a homey yet stylish atmosphere. Our kitchen accessory pack includes a variety of different textures and materials. We've mixed old-world wood, industrial metal, and colorful plastic to achieve our goal. One might snicker at the thought of this fusion, but when you look at it all together you'll become a believer.

FACING PAGE, TOP Take one Hostess Cake kitchen box, throw in a pillow, and finish with cut off table legs. The result: a bed befitting a princess pup.

FACING PAGE, BOTTOM A crusty worktable fitted with a new set of slick red wheels will make you slam on your brakes to get a closer look.

Mudroom Maximus

A Wabash fire door, a hatchery piece, and some other junking nuts and bolts unite forces to keep the family organized.

FACING PAGE, RIGHT This decrepit locker found in a salvage yard was sand-blasted and powder coated to put it back in action. The nostalgia of the knobs and numbers remains.

The game plan for the well redefined kitchen should not be the player left on the bench. Again, form and function had to share the field, no grandstanding allowed. Tile floors, a beautiful color paint (yet fingerprint friendly), and a practical assortment of useful junk were put together to form this winning team.

BIG STORAGE

The locker unit, unearthed at a local metal salvage yard is the first-string quarterback. After applying a little TLC, we believe this thing could live to see another hundred years. The Wabash fire door was a find at twenty bucks. We made it handy by attaching a chick transporter (no, really, for young hens) to corral odds and ends and by screwing in nuts and bolts for keys. We think this is what coming home should be all about!

JUNKFO:
Junk is like ice cream, you can settle for flea market shopping (the plain vanilla), or start your own flavor of the month junk calendar and pop into places like your local salvage yard for a scoop of fresh ideas.

Don't worry guys, keep your seats—we've got this one.

A fire door reborn as a pit stop for stuff. Attach a chick transporter, the metal dividers for shelves, and vintage nuts and bolts. Go ahead, get organized!

ABOVE LEFT A tried-and-true vintage doorknob coatrack with a twist—a set of door plates to anchor the knobs.

ABOVE Do you have leftover nuts and bolts lying around the house? Put them to work for you as key holders.

Enhancing a room with good bones is when the party starts. After the palette is prepared, dress it up with some flirty junk projects. Who says you can't have both fun and function? We say have your cake and eat it, too!

SYSTEMATIZE YOUR LIFE

Get it all together with a few simple organizational junk ideas. A coatrack fashioned from doorknobs and recycled wood is hung on the wall from vintage door plates. Just wait—your kiddies will be hanging up their own coats on this little number without reminders from Mom and Dad. An aged stool is great to pull up and take a load off while you lace up those boots before heading out. Quick, take one last look in the mirror before you leave the house. In this case, we suggest a new mirror—with an old one you may not catch the lipstick on your teeth.

Finished Hallway

Make it
p. 189

This long hallway leading to the laundry room and the room for relief was an important part of the addition. The Haskins brood wanted more space in the kitchen for a pantry, so the laundry room needed to be uprooted. Another issue was the absence of a must-have powder room. We conquered both problems in one swoop.

The first stop in the hall is the newly built laundry facility we lovingly named "the missing sock." It is small, but very functional. Stop number two (no pun intended), the powder room located at the end by the window.

Our cast-off creations include metal window frames (most likely from a farm outbuilding) used to display kids' artwork, a once creepy, old sewing table (ten bucks), and a lovely wood window recycled from another room in the house. By the way, don't miss the metal mesh atop the wall, constructed to let the sunshine in.

Make it p. 190

← *Style Tweak*

Instead of metallic spray paint and corrugated metal on your new hall table, refinish the wood in a warm tone and attach a scrap of architectural molding to the front for a more traditional flavor.

ABOVE Three metal window frames all in a row display kids' artwork, designed for easy in and out replacement. Artwork is a parent's pride and nightmare at the same time. Display, throw, and replace. Three simple rules to live by.

FACING PAGE We found a wooden window hidden in a closet. Attached with Velcro above the sewing table, it added just the right touch of eye candy.

DELECTABLE DINING

THE MUSGJERDS

TWIN TODDLERS

BRIGHT FUTURE

MANY SINGLE
FRIENDS

STARTER HOME

Gleaming hardwood floors, classic windows with chubby molding, and customary corner cupboards are all good things. Traditional trappings, not so good; at least not for our family of four with a more contemporary mind-set. No worries, a home with movie star bone structure does not confine you to stodgy styling.

To solve the homeowners' catch-22, we exercised a galvanized plan of attack. Black and white polka dots, timeless but not tired, became our muse for this project. Once our "T"s were crossed and our "I"s dotted, we spiffed up the walls with a fresh coat of white and threw in a bright green accent color just for fun.

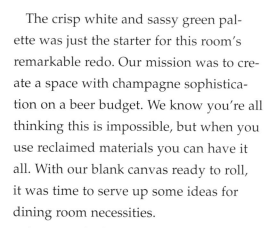

The crisp white and sassy green palette was just the starter for this room's remarkable redo. Our mission was to create a space with champagne sophistication on a beer budget. We know you're all thinking this is impossible, but when you use reclaimed materials you can have it all. With our blank canvas ready to roll, it was time to serve up some ideas for dining room necessities.

A trip to the local building reuse center turned out to be very rewarding. We found most of the makings for the entrees in the room, not to mention a couple of sides. Now that's what we call one-stop junking. After that, it was off to our favorite Swedish discount furniture megastore, don'cha know, in search of the finishing touches. The green office chairs we found were an excellent fit. They were the perfect color, the right price, and had circle cutouts to boot. Yee haw!

3 WISHES

Contemporary Cantina

Drinks on the House

Cappuccino Corner

We're well-known for thinking more than just a little outside the box, and this buffet is a fine example of the way we operate. These sweet little ditties were our first find at the reuse center. A mere fifteen dollars per sink pedestal produced a quirky yet functional buffet sure to break the ice at any dinner party. Next, we had glass cut to fit, and secured it with surface protectors to curtail any problems with slippage. Finally, a few tabletop dressings to refine the look. From loo to dining hall, that's how we define repurposing.

FACING PAGE, LEFT Vintage paper will enhance just about any room. This sign had "dining room" written all over it.

FACING PAGE, RIGHT Pedestal sink bases in a variety of shapes and sizes join the food service industry. We built bases to even up the heights.

LEFT This wall sconce is fusion at its best: a new metal wall piece spiced up with old soap dishes for candles.

Contemporary Cantina

Make it p. 191

KODAK E100VS

44   45

BEFORE

JUNKFO:

While shopping flea markets, search out vendors who are hardware specialists. Follow this piece of rainbow advice and you will find your own personal pot of hinges.

FACING PAGE Here we performed the ultimate "opposites attract" marriage ceremony. Very traditional surroundings and ultra mod furnishings are perfect life partners.

ABOVE LEFT For a great placecard holder, pick a hinge that bends in just the right place so that it stands at attention.

ABOVE RIGHT Gauges with flat glass tops are ideal candle holders. For fun, pair a gauge with a magnifying glass.

Our cute couple loved the character their newly acquired classic charmer provided, but wanted an interior design package that reflected their modern-style preferences. This request seemed easy enough, but with two baby boys on board practicality needed to be considered. Junk came to the rescue bringing livable yet tastefully trendy decor.

To balance the whimsical sideboard, we needed a streamlined dining table. Our second and third great snags at the reuse center provided the basis for our design. An old door as a tabletop has been done before, but, we dare say, not this well. When hooked up with a set-aside exten-

sion ladder and some reclaimed molding the end result is spectacular. Brush on some slick black paint and it's time to call everyone for dinner.

HARDWORKING JUNK

Industrial junk is definitely working overtime on this table. We integrated polished metal junk, happening discount dishware, and spunky napkins to establish this chic dinner party at Old Country buffet prices. In fact, if you take this route, you'll actually have money to spare for food!

Sweet Details

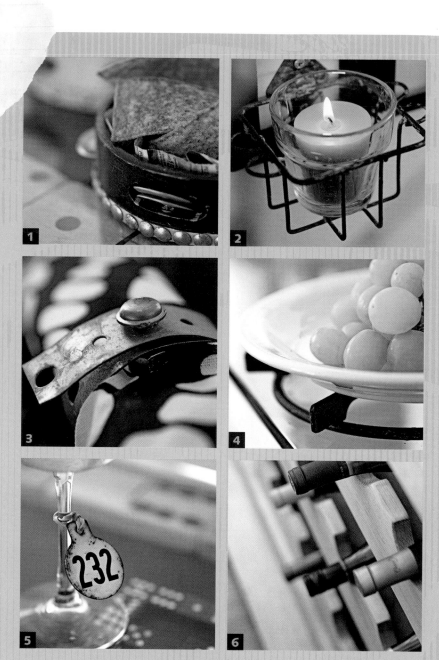

1. **SERVE UP YOUR CHIPS** in a tambourine for a look that is music to the ears.

2. **THESE HOLDERS** were designed for soap, but are a lot more interesting as candle holders.

3. **ONE MIGHT BOLT** strapping tape together for offbeat napkin holders. Don't forget to clip the bolt on the inside to avoid snagging napkins.

4. **STORE-BOUGHT TRIVETS** aren't all that cool, so try slipping a repurposed stove grate under your plates instead.

5. **SOMETIMES YOU FIND** a piece of junk and you have no idea what it was. Don't fret—you can always make it something else, like a wineglass charm.

6. **NO ROOM FOR A WINE CELLAR?** Keep bottles on hand in a redesigned radiator cover.

Seating is key when designing a modern space. As you know, we often go for the mixed bag of chairs around a table, but in this space it wasn't appropriate. The clean lines of the Swedish furniture megastore chairs only required one junk companion.

We found some leftover stool tops back at the shop and returned them to the table as none other than a stool for two. Imagine that! The stool base was crafted from excess building supplies and sized to fit the wooden disks. Yes, this makes for great seating, but if the homeowners tire of it there, they can always employ it as a mod coffee table.

1

JUNKER'S JUJU

A clean, simple, and straight-forward design methodology is crucial when moving in a contemporary direction. You'll notice we didn't go wild with color, but what we did do was introduce a punchy accent shade. The polka-dot rug speaks for itself.

2

1. PAINTS

Again, we're keeping it simple. Benjamin Moore's Atrium White is always a good choice (and our pick for the walls and trim) when you're after a crisp white. If you are looking for a softer shade of white, Benjamin Moore's Linen White is a safe bet. To provide the needed punch, we selected Benjamin Moore's Palisades Park (inside corner cupboards) to coordinate with the dining chairs.

2. POLKA DOTS

The polka-dot resurgence of the 1980s just may be outdone by this one. Yes, they're baaaack! The big, bold, and beautiful pattern is a promi-nent design element in this room. The natural fiber rug provides the ying to the polka dots' yang.

3. STUFF

Hardware to a junker is like a diamond to a girl, BFF. Hinges, members of the hardware family, are employed in this chapter as placecard holders, but check out page 7 for another fun idea.

3

Drinks on the House

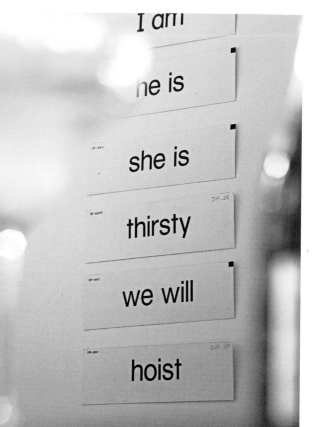

ABOVE LEFT Old lawn dominos outline the edge of the bar top while the indoor variety denotes the reason for celebration.

ABOVE RIGHT These old-school flash cards provide the comic relief typically found in the greeting card aisle at the drug-store.

Our resident couple adores spending time with their get-up-and-go twin boys, but they also look forward to parents' time out. Therefore, it came as no surprise when this Mom and Dad requested a place to enjoy an adult beverage from time to time. As hardworking junk experts and parents ourselves, we were totally on top of this cry for help.

THE DOMINO EFFECT

The shells of two radiator covers lost their screens to a project that appears in another room in the book (see page 77). We couldn't let the shells go to waste, so they became the frames for our bar and wine storage cabinet. The units were functional, but they needed some pizzazz. Dominoes, our graphic dotted friends, added the perfectly playful garnish.

I am

he is

she is

thirsty

we will

hoist

Black computer
mouse pads as wall
decor worked well
with our overall
inexpensive, but chic
decorating initiative.

Look what fun these two kids are having as they are just about to dive into their yummy frozen concoctions. We helped them out with their party room needs by filling the empty frame of a radiator cover with racks to hold twelve wine bottles and enough glass storage for a small gathering with friends. Salud!

The pocket-size space we had to work with was long, narrow, and heavily windowed. In order to make the room appear more spacious, we needed to be mindful of the scale of the furnishings. The two radiator covers were perfectly proportionate and fit nicely against the wall on one side of the room.

TOP LEFT After the chips are gone and you've enjoyed a margarita, play along with the music. "Mr. Tambourine Man" never sounded so good.

LEFT This glass top is removable, so keep a bowl of dominoes handy and feel free to express yourself.

FACING PAGE, RIGHT These two knuckleheads are smiling from ear to ear because their room makeover cost less than their monthly diaper bill.

Style Tweak

We applied a clear coat of stain to the wood wine racks for a modish feel. If you want to achieve a seductive, smokey cigar bar look reminiscent of the 1940s, finish the shelves with deep, rich brown and cover the tops with solid wood.

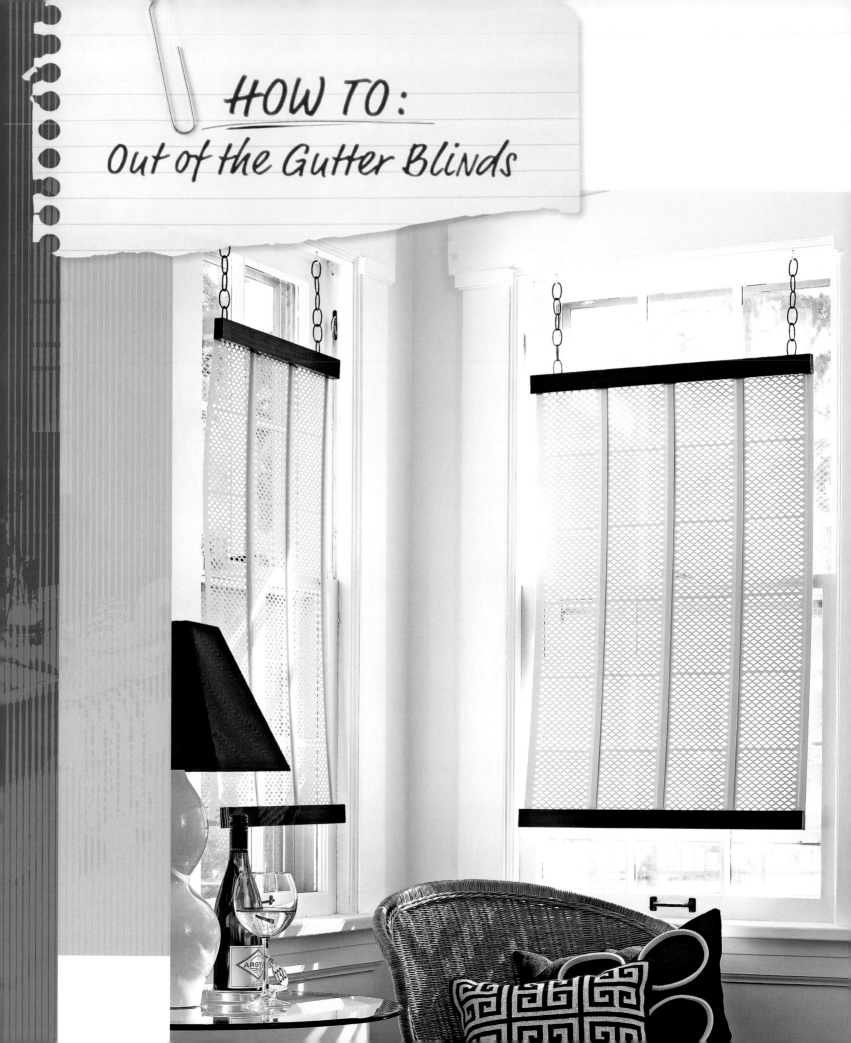

HOW TO:
Out of the Gutter Blinds

Plastic rain gutter covers generously left behind by the previous homeowners were discovered in the garage. We had no need for them outside, so decided to cover windows rather than gutters. Now that is resourceful.

MATERIALS NEEDED

- 1 x 2 pine board
- Plastic rain gutter protectors
- Easy cable clips
- Eye hooks
- Lightweight black metal chain

TOOLS NEEDED

- Junker's Toolbox (see page 185)

METHOD

1. Connect gutter protectors to fit window size widthwise (We used 4.) Ⓐ.
2. Cut to fit and paint 2 pieces of 1 x 2 pine board to finish top and bottom edge of each blind Ⓑ.
3. Attach finished wood pieces to gutter protectors with small screws Ⓒ.
4. Attach easy cable clips to wood frame.
5. Measure and cut metal chain for your window so that the blind is centered in the window.
6. Screw eye hooks into inside of window frame.
7. Connect chain to window frame, then suspend from eye hooks.

Cappuccino
Corner

I'm putting plastic in a window and I'm darn proud of it!

LEFT Plastic may be cheap, but it doesn't have to look it. Our blinds didn't break the bank and they added an unexpected element to the mix.

BELOW Two crusty, warehouse light covers were introduced to a welder, then a can of white spray paint. The finished product is one nifty side table.

At the conclusion of a party or even the morning just before, there's nothing like a place to sit, relax, and have a welcome cup of coffee. Our cute café is suited up with affordable wicker chairs, cushy pillows, and a table à la junk.

TABLE FOR TWO

The table is constructed from light covers from a warehouse turned end to end and welded together using new steel supports. A couple coats of white paint were applied and a ready-made glass round to complete the table. Now, it's high time to turn the lights out in this chapter and move on to the next.

FACING PAGE Whether you're enjoying a glass of wine after work or a cup of coffee at daybreak, a sunlit nook is a great place to kick back.

LAUNDRY LOUNGE

THE LEMMERMANS
....
2 TEENS + 1 PRE-
TEEN = MANY
COSTUME
CHANGES

HARDWORKING
MOM AND DAD

VICTORIAN
FARMHOUSE
....

Cast your eyes upon this inviting, multi-functional family laundromat. The space is small, but with some inventive thinking and a bunch of junk, we were able to get the wrinkles out. We received a laundry list of requests from our homeowners beyond just getting the clothes clean. Mom is a seamstress and the wrapper of gifts; Dad needed a place to put his dirty work clothes and keep his robe close at hand for after a soak in the hot tub nearby. As for the kids, they thought that as long as Mom and Dad were happy, they wouldn't be turning to the youngsters for help with the laundry.

The rest of this home is a lovingly restored Victorian farmhouse, so you can imagine our surprise when we saw the laundry room—like the messy closet you close the door on before company shows up. For more than a few, this is the last place you think about fixing up. The Family L, too, had fairly ignored this space.

But these rooms should not be forgotten—just stop and consider for a moment how much time you spend doing laundry. Actually, you might want to hold up there and just take our word that everyone deserves a laundry room like this new and improved model.

CLEAR THE DECKS

Although the old laundry facility was pretty functional, it needed some added charm to flow with the rest of the home. Our first task was to create a clean slate, so for starters we disposed of the navy laminate countertops and cabinets, then painted over the busy, patterned walls with a neutral shade that provided a more pristine atmosphere. After that, completing the job was a snap. New upper cabinets were installed and the doors were removed from the lower cabinets. All were painted a bright white. A natural wood surface replaced the tacky blue laminate. The missing country charisma was now firmly in place.

BEFORE

3 WISHES

Laundromat

Crafty Corner

Stowage

FACING PAGE, LEFT Don't get hung up by difficùlt projects. A hanger with no pants makes a wonderful picture hook.

FACING PAGE, RIGHT This room needed a presoak, hot wash, and heavy-duty dry to make it crisp and clean.

LEFT Serger thread stands at the ready in a $5 cosmetic case we found at a neighborhood garage sale.

Laundromat

Soft, neutral colors accented with metal accessories left this laundry room looking squeaky clean.

FACING PAGE, BOTTOM Long, thin pieces of wood with too few supporting brackets left these shelves a little saggy. Look out below!

LEFT We've told you all along that as a junker you need to have a sense of humor. A farmer's meat drying rack turned laundry room organizer? Now that's hysterical.

BELOW Vintage locker baskets are on our top ten list of great junk. If you need to contain it, a locker basket is your best bet.

Dressing up a washer and dryer is no easy task. Let's face it, boys and girls, they just aren't that attractive. So when you decide to tackle this job keep the word "playful" in mind. Our aim was to provide open storage and keep it interesting. When we dug this meat drying rack (hooks and all) out of an old barn, we knew we had our answer. And since we already had a supply of locker baskets on hand, we knew we had our storage containers, too.

HOOK ME UP

After installing the meat rack, we attached the baskets to the lower board with pieces of a measuring stick. The tips of the meat

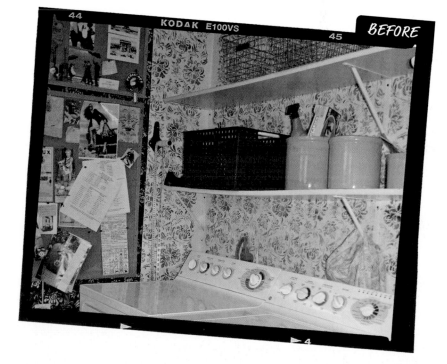

KODAK E100VS

BEFORE

hooks were sharp, so to avoid any bloodshed, we affixed bits and pieces of metal junk to each tip with an epoxy, JB Weld®. To complete the washer-dryer ensemble, we replaced the plastic washtub with a cooler vintage model.

How do you go about selecting junk for a particular room? First and foremost, trust your instincts. If you are drawn to a piece and it's affordable, buy it. Second, make a list of needs for your space before you hit the junking trail. This will help not only to keep you focused, but will open your mind to imaginative thinking. Third, forget about what something was, and think about what it could become.

If you arm yourself with these three pieces of advice (and your ATM card), you will enjoy a whole new shopping experience. How do you think we came up with a meat drying rack for laundry storage? See, it works!

Sweet Details

1. **A CHICKEN FEEDER** relieved of its original duty now shines brightly as a ceiling fixture.

2. **NOTHING SAYS CRUSTY** like an old glass bottle.

3. **WRINGING LAUNDRY DRY** by hand sure was fun, but sad to say those days have passed. This obsolete dryer now enjoys new life as a towel rack.

4. **TIN BOXES** are great for storing those items that aren't aesthetically pleasing. Better yet, make labels for them with vintage wallpaper.

5. **WHY SHOULD THIS PIECE OF TRASH** be limited to holding pants and skirts straight? We let it spread its clampers and soar to new heights as a picture holder.

6. **CRAFTY PEOPLE** need crafty containers like this vented metal drawer.

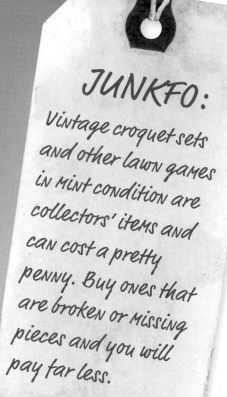

JUNKFO: Vintage croquet sets and other lawn games in mint condition are collectors' items and can cost a pretty penny. Buy ones that are broken or missing pieces and you will pay far less.

LEFT Remove the croquet mallets and slide in a mop and broom. It's that easy.

JUNKER'S JUJU

Try out this combination of paints, fabrics, and stuff from the junk pile for a laundry room that's farm fresh.

1. STUFF

A great combo of textures played well off the soft and dreamy color scheme for this room. Metal baskets, warm woods, patterned linoleum, and crusty bottles are just a few of the junk components. Number 1 Junk Find? The Five Minute Home Cleaner—originally touted as a hand-washer for your unmention-ables—dispenses detergent.

2. PAINTS

Light paint will help a small space feel much larger. We chose a soft, neutral color palette as our backdrop for this room. The ceiling is painted Devine Whip and the walls are a yummy Devine Sand. This achromatic color selection is based on the color of eggs freshly harvested from the henhouse.

3. FABRICS

We stuck to neutrals again to fit the theme. Lightweight quilting fabrics were the selection of the day. In the window and the lower cabinets, these textiles give you that easy, breezy allure of sheets hung on the clothesline to dry.

Now that this is carcass-free, let's put it in the laundry room.

②

③

Crafty
Corner

Make it
p. 192

Make it
p. 192

Style Tweak

Cotton quilting fabric was the perfect pick for farmhouse window dressings. If you lean more toward whimsical decor, we suggest choosing a bright awning stripe or another bold pattern for your draperies—or you can swap out the lace trim for a less fussy finish.

With three kids in the house, this crafty corner is a busy place. Apparently, farm living provides more than its fair share of rips and tears throughout the course of a day. The center of the long counter was an obvious choice for the sewing station. The top of the counter is constructed of recycled floorboard, so we had to come up with a flat surface for sewing—voilá, a fabulous piece of old linoleum was the answer to our prayers.

IT'S A WRAP

When the sewing is done it's time to wrap the gifts. (There truly is no rest for the weary.) Teenagers tend to have active social lives, so gift-giving becomes part of the routine. We neatly corralled wrapping paper in a wire bin. The twine and string are also close by on a tidy junk holder.

FACING PAGE Wimpy molding is out of place in an old farmhouse. To put this room back in the proper era, we beefed up the trim in a big way.

TOP A redesigned small tool displayer from an old hardware store makes a handy-dandy thread bearer.

LEFT Breezy drapery panels hang from ice box hinges. You have to love that.

HOW TO:
Leaded glass twine holder

Our scrap wood pieces may vary from those stowed in your workshop. If you don't have a "preowned" cabinet door on hand, any sturdy board will do. If it is raw wood, paint and distress it for an old-world finish.

MATERIALS NEEDED

- Vintage cabinet door or other solid wood piece
- Window glass divided by leading
- 5 hinge pins (We used old, standard 4 in., but they can be cut to size.)
- Flat shoe or quarter round trim, about 26 in. to 30 in.
- Loose joint adhesive that will swell the wood.

TOOLS NEEDED

- Junker's Toolbox (see page 185)

METHOD

1. Cut door or wood to size for three balls of twine (ours was 5 in. by 9 in.).
2. Nail or glue legs to bottom (we used scrap wood from the cabinet door).
3. Cut trim to fit edges and nail on with brads.
4. Measure and drill holes across center for hinge pins.
5. Drill holes in each of the back corners of wood Ⓐ.
6. Apply joint adhesive to each hole and insert hinge pin Ⓑ.
7. Slip window onto back hinge pin Ⓒ.

Stowage

Make a decorating statement by choosing interesting items to store your necessities, such as our metal basket for towels.

FACING PAGE, LEFT
Bi-fold doors are a pet peeve of ours. This door was still functional, so we just made it look better by inserting old radiator screen.

FACING PAGE, RIGHT
Outdoor faucet handles are like rabbits—they seem to multiply—so now's as good a time as any to call a welder and put together a tubular coatrack.

Quick Draw McWhitney, the fastest glue gun in the Midwest.

Storage in this multipurposed room was an issue. We needed new upper cabinets and cover-ups for those below. The draperies with farm charm on the lower cabinets were elementary, but the real artistry is in the uppers. Adding character to this room was essential. A salvage store yielded a cabinet we loved, but it didn't fit the space.

A CUT-AND-DRIED SOLUTION

This didn't deter us for long. We just cut the cabinet in two. The one closest to the bulletin board is two thirds of the original, and the other is the remaining portion. Brilliant! Next, we installed them, then added ceiling molding and painted. Another storage victory.

MAKING AN ENTRANCE

THE SKARTVEDTS

FAMILY FOUR-PACK

TWO FUTURE OLYMPIANS

COLONIAL CHARMER, CIRCA 1890

We think of the mudroom as the collection plate of the home. Its calling is to accommodate a variety of necessary household odds and ends—including the spare change. And this coats-on, coats-off station has got to help the rest of the house run smoothly. Imagine mornings as our family foursome departs for work, school, or weekend activities. If the room is not ready to receiveith, then neither is our family, and we couldn't have that!

The Skartvedts' request was standard organization without standard-issue furniture and accessories. It was time for a junk intervention to reinstate peace amid the morning madness.

We adore metal baskets because they have so many different uses. Here we have put one to work as a tableware tote.

3 WISHES
The Family Cupboard

Mirror, Mirror on the Wall

Catchall Caddy

Build it and the boots will come.

Looks like the junk fairies have been at it again. We began by emptying the entire room to see what we had to work with. Then we beefed up the molding to add character, painted the walls and ceiling a cheery color to create a sense of spaciousness, and dropped in cork flooring, which is durable and easy on the feet.

MESS MANAGEMENT 101
Most families have a lot of stuff to contend with in a mudroom and our family was no different. To plan your own fantasy mudroom, start by making a list of everything that needs to be stored, then divide the list into groups to help identify the furniture pieces and storage units needed.

Then it's off to acquire suitable junk. In our case, the Skartvedts needed a large cupboard; storage for kids' toys, shoes, picnic gear; and something for the boots and coats. Follow these simple guidelines and, before you know, it your mess will be manageable.

Style Tweak

Can you believe we actually used this piece for its intended purpose? But you don't have to. If you choose pretty over purpose, remove the coats and hang mason jars filled with sand and candles from the coat hooks. Place the candle holder outside the mudroom door for ambient lighting.

The Family Cupboard

BOYS

GIRLS

FACING PAGE This is what we call "everything in a nutshell." A hold-it-all cabinet with coatracks alongside make for a streamlined mudroom.

LEFT Can we have your attention, boys? Please keep your stuff on your side of the cabinet and we will do the same.

BOTTOM Boots and shoes find refuge from the storm under the shelter of the family storage cabinet.

We thought gender-specific storage areas would be a novel idea for this mudroom. Seeing that we were in possession of these awesome grade school restroom signs, we decided to take a run at it. We came across this cabinet top at a building reuse center and knew instantly that with just a few alterations it would work well as a storage unit. A base was added to give more height and provide shelving for footwear.

One side of the cabinet was assigned to Mom and daughter while reserving the other half for the boys' more aromatic sports gear. (We're always thinking of the men.) Seriously, behind closed doors a myriad of plug-ugly equipment can be kept out of sight and still be readily accessible. Everything from picnic blankets to car cleaners are packed behind these doors.

The cabinet was given a boost by adding two new shelves at the bottom, one for shoes and one for boots, which really need breathing room. The top shelf was constructed with wood slats and the bottom with metal mesh allowing boots to dry. This old-world version is practical and pretty. Next to the boots is a handy-dandy picnic basket packed and ready to go. Stuff one of your own with all the nuts and bolts for a picture-perfect family gathering. With one of these on hand, all you need to worry about is the food.

HOW TO:
Hand drill coatrack

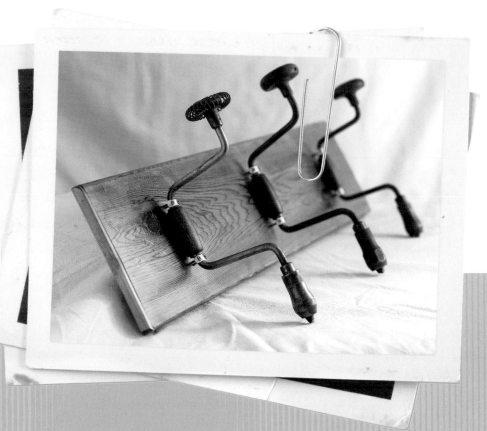

Like so much other old stuff, these handsome hand drills were built to last, so we gave them a reason to carry on.

MATERIALS NEEDED

- Three vintage hand drills
- Recycled pine floorboard or new 1 x 8 board
- Small trim board
- 6 plastic fasteners
- Medium colored stain

TOOLS NEEDED

- Junker's Toolbox (see page 185)

METHOD

1. Measure and cut recycled floorboard or new wood to fit your space. (Ours is approximately 36 in.)
2. If using recycled floorboard, scribe curve of board onto trim piece and cut following your line. Do one for each end of the board Ⓐ.
3. Sand the trim pieces to smooth the rounded cuts Ⓑ.
4. Attach trim pieces with finishing nails, one to each end of the floorboard.
5. Stain trim to match floorboard or stain the new board and trim a medium tone.
6. Measure and place hand drills an equal distance from one another on the board.
7. Attach hand drills to floorboard or new board with plastic fasteners Ⓒ.

Mirror, Mirror on the Wall

LEFT Flowers are always a nice touch, but not always practical. If you're fresh out of flowers, put feathers in the test tubes instead.

Every gorgeous room begins with a little trim.

Make it
p. 193

Make it
p. 193

Mirror, mirror on the wall, who's the fairest of them all? Well, we know it's not the queen, and Dopey is definitely out of the running. So you are the fairest of your own domain. Keeping that in mind, when you're on your way out the door or coming home to greet your family, there is no harm in looking your best. A well-equipped mudroom needs a place to make sure you're looking good.

The corner of the room next to the door was prime real estate for a makeup station. Two salvaged boot stretchers and an out-of-service restaurant tray make a wonderful wall-mounted table. A vintage mirror that was found in the garage com-

plete the fluff-and-buff ensemble. In addition, the station works well for outgoing and incoming mail, notes, and reminders. If anyone is running short on cash they can grab some change on their way out the door. Multipurpose units like this table are essential when working with small spaces. Remember, the more functions one piece can perform the better it is.

On top of being a hard worker, this wall table is a crafty space saver essential to small areas. If we went with a floor model, traffic would get clogged from entry to the main living area of the home. Also, without table legs on the floor, there's room for footwear overflow.

TOP LEFT On the wall adjacent to our boot form tray, an old broom holder was the perfect custodian for laboratory test tubes and spring tulips.

TOP RIGHT How this cherry pitter worked was a mystery to us, so to keep things easy we used it to hold pocket change.

The mudroom is the family portal from the indoors to the outdoors. Our desire was to capture the easy, breezy look and feel of a gorgeous spring day.

1. PAINTS

To achieve this, we selected a beautiful grayed down sky shade, Benjamin Moore Wyeth Blue, for the primary color. The ceiling color was softened by mixing equal parts of Wyeth Blue with white. The accent color on the door, Benjamin Moore Greenfield Pumpkin, is bold yet warm and inviting.

2. FABRICS

We used a host of ready-made pillows, store-bought window coverings, and an off-the-rack rug. Here's a tip. When shopping for new accessories don't limit yourself to one store. Our shopping tour included several different retailers. All items were purchased at reasonable prices, and in some cases were closeout items. We encourage mixing and matching junk with the new stuff.

3. JUNK METAL

Junk hailing from the metal underworld is among our favorite. As you can see, we have used a medley to enhance this room. Remember there is no law against mixing stainless with brass. The corroded brass hardware piece used to hang keys complements the shiny stainless coatrack. Throw in an iron grate for good measure and you will have composed a symphony.

①

②

③

JUNKER'S JUJU

Catchall Caddy

This corner grouping is another good example of making the most out of the room you have. Using vacant wall space for storage in a clever container is both functional and attractive.

Make it p. 194

Every family we know, large or small, needs a place to collect and neatly contain all of those tiny little objects that tend to get misplaced—garage door openers, flashlights, and cell phones to name a few frequent offenders. Sound familiar? Unless you want to invest in multiple clappers to locate your on-the-lamb necessities, we highly recommend that you consider this less expensive and headache free alternative.

RESTORAGE

An antique Swedish wooden crate in disrepair was lovingly restored and enhanced to act as our family's keeper of the small stuff. A little wood cleaner and some shelving constructed from scrap wood brought the outmoded crate back from the scrap pile to provide the answer to our storage woes. A few pieces of hardware attached at the top for hanging items and we were rolling full steam ahead. The only thing left was to fill it up and that was no challenge.

We were able to crate and store all of the family's elfin essentials with room to spare. We even managed to squeeze in a tailor-made first-aid kit perfect for making the kids' boo-boos go bye-bye.

BOTTOM LEFT A large grate rescued from a salvage yard works well as a boot dryer. Slip in castors to raise it off the floor.

BOTTOM RIGHT Attending to minor cuts and mosquito bites is child's play when you have a homespun first-aid kit on hand.

DRIP-DRY BOOTS

We had vacant floor space below the storage crate that was begging for an assignment. No problem, ask and you shall receive. A large iron grate with decorative cutouts was an obvious choice to carry the burden of boot drying. It needed to be raised off the floor in order to work properly, so we enlisted the help of four porcelain castors that we attached to each of the grates' four corners. If you wish, throw a sheet of heavy duty plastic under the dryer to save wear and tear on the floor.

We know from experience that boot drying is messy business, so we added the castors for function and good looks, too. They provide a convenient roll-on, roll-off feature allowing for easy cleaning of the drip pad below, leaving us all with more time to play.

Sweet Details

1. **YOU WON'T FIND HANDLES** like these on a new piece of furniture, so go for the junk whenever possible.

2. **A PIECE OF HARDWARE** with hard-earned patina makes for a great key holder.

3. **THIS METAL TOTE** is prepared to go straight from the cabinet to the picnic table.

4. **EMBELLISH YOUR STORE-BOUGHT** napkin rings with upholstery tacks and watch keys.

5. **SUPER BALLS®** in a vase are far more original than the predictable pile of rocks.

6. **AN APPLE PRESS** with a few minor adjustments lights up the mudroom.

JUNKFO: This handle is a work of art. It could be salvaged for a different purpose, such as a drawer pull or a doorknob on a large armoire.

LEFT The handle of this hand-powered drill is almost too pretty to be covered with a hanging coat.

LIVING ROOM LUXURY

Do you remember back in the day when the living room was a place you only looked at but never dared to enter? The times when you dreamed of sitting on that perfectly pristine, plastic-covered sofa that was reserved for Mom's bridge club? Those days are long gone, so out with the stuffy and in with the comfy.

Our more casual lifestyles have redefined the way we use our living rooms. After a long day at the salt mines, it's wonderful to be welcomed home by a room that is comforting to weary working souls, but also ready to receive family and friends— even if they weren't invited.

This was a small space, so our furniture pieces needed to be selected with extra care. Two small sofas provided maximum seating.

Living areas should be comfortable as well as beautiful. For example, over-sized, white slip-covered sofas with lots of stuffing will provide both elements to your room. Throw in a beat up old coffee table constructed from scrap wood and an iron gate, and you will have firmly established a junking good look of your own. However, furniture alone does not complete a room, it's just a good place to start. For example, the neutral color scheme also played an important role in this makeover. The combination of several soft shades of off-white on textured walls added a European flavor.

THE ARTIFACTOR

Days gone by and the memories they've made should not be left out of the lovely picture in which you dwell. You have chosen your furniture pieces, so take care to include cherished heirlooms from your families' pasts. A stunning architectural remnant from Grandma Rose, vintage family photos showing off those fabulous 1940s dippity-do hairstyles, and an eye-catching floral arrangement will dress a window quite nicely. When accessorizing your space, keep in mind that more is not always merrier.

TOP LEFT The origin of the white architectural remnant included in this window vignette is unknown, but we do know it's spectacular.

TOP RIGHT The fireplace surround was too small and constructed with a mishmash of materials that desperately needed blending.

Room to Read

function. You guessed it! After work, they needed a tranquil arena to kick back, relax, read, and enjoy a few well-deserved moments of uninterrupted quiet time. It sounds too good to be true, doesn't it? We're happy to say it is not. After casting aside our own doubts, we found a way to make their dreams come true.

DIVIDE AND CONQUER

Somewhere along the junking highway, we discovered that rooms are like children. They both need well-established boundaries. That's exactly what we did here. By repositioning the chairs to face each other and placing a table in between, we achieved separate spaces that still relate to each other. We also did away with any unnecessary furniture and reorganized the bookcases to free the space from frenzy. Remember, soft border

One of our dashing duo's dreams was to have an invigorating space in which to greet each day and share a cup of coffee before heading out for the grind. On the flip side, they wanted this same space to perform a very separate

LEFT The bookcases in this room are the obvious focal point, so we kept the furniture and accents subdued.

TOP Wheel in a wonderfully worn cart from a flourmill and repurpose it as a coffee table with character, like we did here.

RIGHT Chipped up ceramic tile trim pieces are picture-perfect for displaying photos of those cherubic little faces that warm your heart.

JUNKFO: Architectural salvage stores are amazing. At first blush, the stuff may seem too rich for your blood, but like at home, there's usually a basement. Check there for hot deals.

control creates definition and balance, so feel free to divide and conquer.

On the other side of the reading ranch, we incorporated more architectural salvage in keeping with the bookish nature of the room. The expansive built-ins were the perfect environment for architectural accessories, but needed a little attention. Most of our pieces were a creamy white, so we painted the inside walls a rich smoky blue to better showcase the junk accoutrement.

COLLECTION CONFECTION

Two junkers in a salvage store can be likened to two kids in a candy store. Take a hint from us. An architectural salvage collection is a yummy confection, but you don't want to get carried away. When selecting your bookcase accessories consider dimension, texture, and color. Varying the sizes and shapes of your pieces will create interest, and a mixture of materials will put the peanut butter in your chocolate.

I didn't swallow a canary; I just found a great piece of junk.

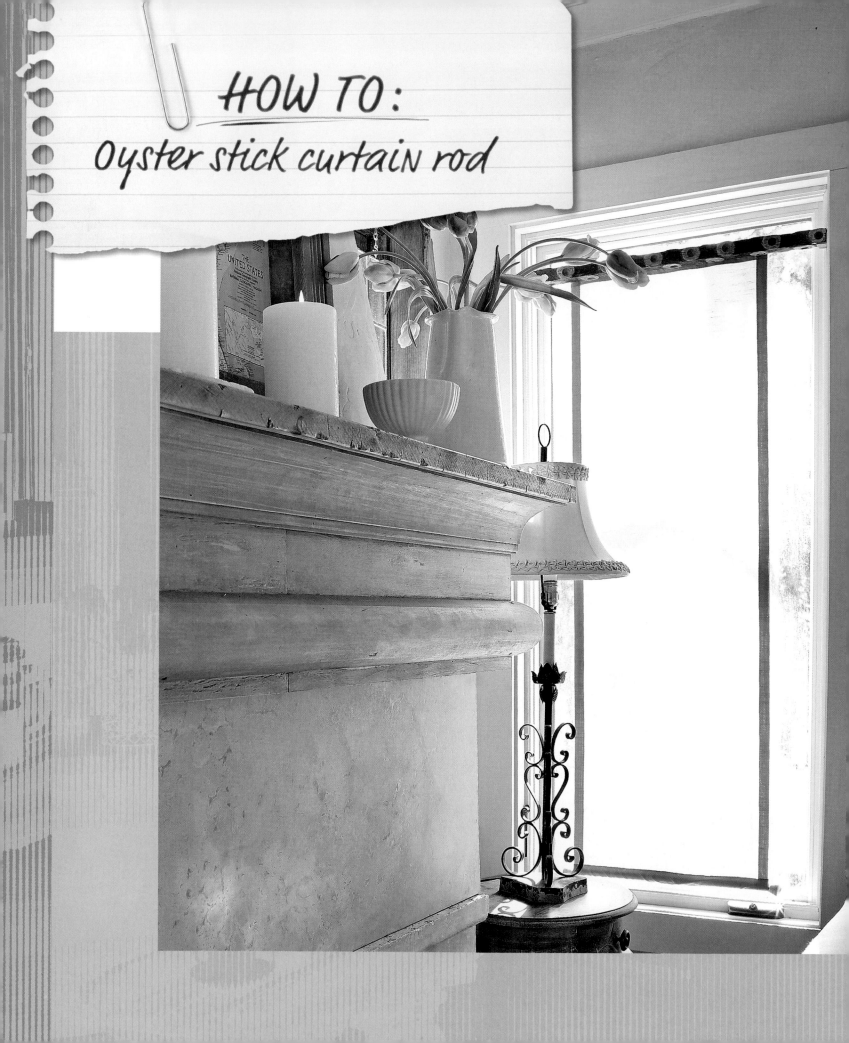

HOW TO:
Oyster stick curtain rod

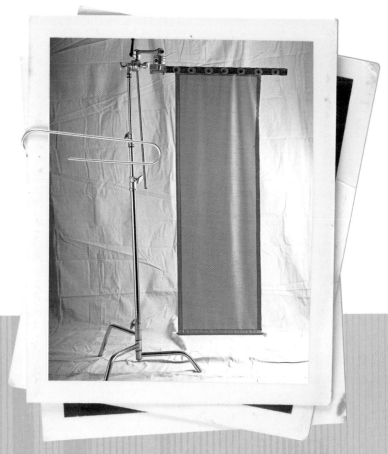

Oyster sticks—used for seeding oyster beds—are unusual to say the least, but perform nicely as curtain rods. If you can't find these, try vintage walking sticks.

MATERIALS NEEDED
- Oyster harvesting sticks or a similar piece of wood
- Heavy-duty double-stick Velcro®
- A small wooden dowel, we used two 2-in. pieces.
- New drawer pulls
- Metal pipe, about 24 in.
- Junk or new hanging brackets

TOOLS NEEDED
- Junker's Toolbox (see page 185)

METHOD
1. Cut metal pipe to fit width of drapery panel Ⓐ.

2. Cut oyster stick or other wooden junk find to fit inside of window, leaving a quarter of an inch leeway so rod will sit comfortably on curtain bracket.

3. Cut Velcro to appropriate length and adhere one side to the oyster harvesting stick and the other to the drapery panel Ⓑ.

4. Cut dowel into two 2-in. sections and screw drawer pulls into dowel sections.

5. Attach top of drapery panel to oyster stick.

6. Insert metal pipe into pocket at the bottom of drapery panel.

7. Insert a drawer pull into each end of the pipe Ⓒ.

8. Screw curtain brackets into window and hang seaworthy window treatments.

Sophisticated Storage

A living room is generally the entertaining space in the home. Avoid overfurnishing to allow space for large gatherings.

This living room is a large, spectacular space with character and charm already on board, but not without its flaws. Its long and narrow dimensions presented design dilemmas. The homeowners wanted to make this room the center of all things good in their home and were at loss as to how to put their plan into action.

One challenge was to give them storage on the QT. Storage in a living room is required, but it shouldn't sing out loud. A quiet hum is more appropriate.

CARGO CONTAINMENT

We're sure you've heard us say it before. Look around and rediscover what you already own and make it work for you. Right before our junking eyes was a dilapidated, yet stunning dresser that was missing its top. A visit to the garage uncovered a tabletop with no base. The result was a sophisticated piece of furniture with plenty of interior cargo space.

BOTTOM LEFT Recap a bureau with an unemployed tabletop and give it a paint job to create a classy storage cupboard.

BOTTOM RIGHT Corbels are the mainstay of architectural salvage. Add a base, some vintage hooks, and you have a handsome picture holder.

Make it
p.196

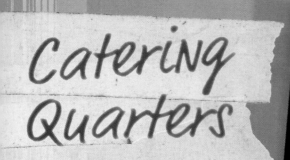

To add a twist to this traditional room we hung contemporary letters in place of a predictable piece of artwork or mirror.

Shiver me timbers, our young lad and lassie have far more going on in their lives than just work. They look forward to entertaining on weekends and holidays with unbridled anticipation. Again, the question was not what was needed, but how to get there. It was time for us to wrestle with wish number three.

First, we flushed out an open area in the center portion of the room, providing space for plenty of friends and family members to mingle, but we still had to devise a butler station for food and beverages. After dividing the room into

vignettes, we were left with only one wall to address this issue. The wall could only handle a long, shallow table that needed to accommodate all of the party favors.

To the rescue, along came a shutter. We cut it in two pieces; one section became the tabletop and the other the lower shelf. Our welder formed a metal frame and we covered both shutter pieces with glass for smooth operating. Whew, another day on the junk pile, another wish granted.

TOP LEFT Dish up your goodies on vintage white iron-stone plates. It's a classic choice for a classic room.

TOP RIGHT This narrow shutter was the ideal subject for a repurposing. Ripped from its outdoor duties, it is now the life of the party.

Looks like Sue knows what she's doing.
Fooled ya!

JUNKER'S JUJU

Soft and subtle was our backdrop of choice, so as to allow plenty of ta-da to unfold in the accent pieces we brought on board this luxury liner living room.

1. PAINTS

A monochromatic color story is always a winning bet when reaching for upmarket appeal. Coat your walls with an understated selection such as Benjamin Moore's Gold Tone, and use the same shade on your molding. If you want to give your wood an appearance of age, you can apply a light coat of stain. Two coats of Smokey Mountain by Benjamin Moore were applied to the inside of the bookcases to showcase the white architectural pieces.

2. JUNK

And by junk we mean architectural salvage. Beautiful scrap wood embellishment pieces can be found by the truckload at flea markets, antique stores, and junk shops. Create a funky piece of junk art by nailing small remnants with larger pieces like drawer fronts and chair legs onto a piece of heavy plywood.

3. FABRICS

Plenty of white joined with a bold stripe found at a fabric outlet center, a simply sumptuous vintage bark cloth remnant, a summer weight suiting material, and a heavenly gold textile chosen for the window treatments all add up to drop-dead gorgeous.

③

Fireplace Makeover

FACING PAGE This fireplace room is refined without being stuffy. The incorporation of junk furnishings and accessories helps to create a liveable environment.

TOP We needed to create easy access to the storage closet. A well-worn door hung from a vintage barn-door roller provided the solution.

First I paint it, then I sand it off. What's wrong with me?

With three wishes granted, there was only one left to bestow. Unlike traditional genies, junk genies go the extra mile. Of course, like most of us, the homeowners wanted a cozy nook to snuggle by a roaring fire. This request seemed simple enough until the call for a larger-than-life plasma television to be housed in this small space reared its ugly head. Seems we had divergent definitions of the word cozy on our hands. The lady of the house had visions of cuddling with her husband in this room. Now we're not saying he didn't have the same desire, but as a multitasker he saw nothing wrong with being up close and personal with forty-six of his favorite football players at the same time. Stay tuned for the resolution of this hot debate.

While contemplating that issue, we did what we do best. We warmed up the space with a combo of junk and new materials. We began by adding beams to the ceiling to add depth. Then the fun began. Concrete is an amazingly versatile medium for homes. We wanted an unconventional rug, so we cut away some of the wood flooring and replaced it with a concrete rug. The scale of the fireplace surround was too small and needed some beefing up. A fusion of distressed wood molding and concrete slabs did the trick.

Style Tweak

← Style Tweak

Traditional surroundings mandated simple elegance in this room. If urban is your thing, substitute the wooden frames with contemporary metal cabinet casings from a used office supply outlet. Replace the ornate light fixture candleholders with ones sporting more modern lines.

This fireplace demanded a facelift with a flair for the dramatic to uphold its position of dominance in the space. Take a closer look at the fireplace surround, hearth, and mantel. The facade is actually three separate materials. The plaster, wood, and concrete converge so well you can't tell where one material stops and another begins. The melding of textures and materials, along with increasing the mass of the surround, took this fireplace from modest to magnificent.

Now, what about that television? Everything was going so well that we refused to allow the television to dominate the room. There was only one place the monstrosity could go: above the elegant fireplace. Out came the sledgehammer and in went the TV. Once the man toy was in place, we framed the opening on three sides with reclaimed molding pieces. An old map was mounted to plywood with the same molding attached at the bottom of the map, which easily slides in as a cover when the television is off, and out when the men of the gridiron come out to play.

LEFT The fireplace makeover included several different media. Wood, concrete, and plaster came together to create one fabulous surface.

BELOW When the fireplace is not in use, beautify it with a European floor grate and hydrangeas in a large ironstone container.

Make it p.195

Ask yourself this question. Do you really want your space to look like you went to a furniture showroom, purchased a five-piece setting with coordinating accessories, and transplanted it "as shown" directly from the sales floor to your room? We hope that you are shaking your head feverishly in defiance of that silly notion. One way to escape that lackluster approach to interior design is to believe in yourself. You have a great sense of style that is unique to your personality. Please embrace diversity, go forth, and junk up your rooms like only you can.

JUNKFO:
Iron gates are easily obtainable at flea markets. Vendors tend to carry junk that is seasonal, so you're more apt to find one of these pieces during the spring and summer seasons.

RIGHT A concrete "area rug" with pressed tin medallion inserts is just one way we take floor coverings to a whole new level.

WHEN YOU LOOK GOOD, YOU FEEL GOOD

Now that you're confident, campers, it's time to make your site something special. When you're out searching for junk, keep an eye open for those items that reflect your designer DNA. Our couple adored the more refined junk, so together we selected items like windows with bubble glass, graceful drawer pulls, and a weathered iron gate. After the old stuff was chosen, we blended it nicely with the new pieces. When we left, the room was looking good and feeling fine!

Sweet Details

1. **DRESSING YOUR WINDOW** doesn't have to mean drapery. Try suspending a metal-cased window.

2. **A FUNKY MID-CENTURY LIGHT** covering can turn a glass vase from ho-hum to ah-ha.

3. **FANCY VINTAGE DRAWER PULLS** are way more fun than ones purchased at a hardware store.

4. **THESE ARCHITECTURAL PIECES** were just too good to pass up. We screwed them to the wall and slipped in ordinary tumblers to hold flowers.

5. **BROKEN CERAMIC TRIM** pieces are like tinker toys for adults.

6. **A COPPER LIGHT FIXTURE** minus its electrical trappings is reassigned to plant detail.

A SUITE BEDROOM

THE WHITNEYS

MOTHER AND
DAUGHTER DUET

TWO PEAS IN A
POD AND A DOG
NAMED LILY

CAPE COD,
CIRCA 1992

Darling Elizabeth, at long last, gets her turn for a junk makeover. You know what they say about the cobbler's children. Maybe the same is true of a junker's daughter. With the rest of the house completed, it was high time to focus on E's bedroom. As a freshman in high school she desired a more urbane atmosphere that would see her through her upper school years. I couldn't have agreed more and was the first to get the paint roller in hand to cover up the bright green stripes, tacky turquoise, and hot orange that E fancied as a tweener. We only had one problem: two strong-willed girls with very different ideas. Could I, the veteran junk designer, and my

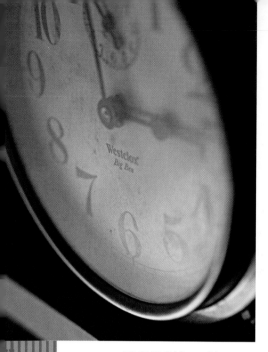

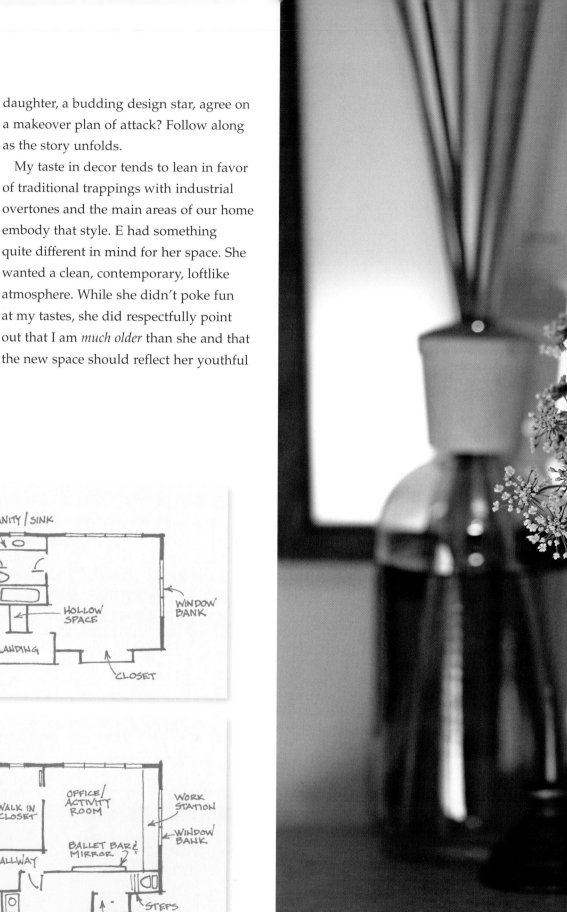

daughter, a budding design star, agree on a makeover plan of attack? Follow along as the story unfolds.

My taste in decor tends to lean in favor of traditional trappings with industrial overtones and the main areas of our home embody that style. E had something quite different in mind for her space. She wanted a clean, contemporary, loftlike atmosphere. While she didn't poke fun at my tastes, she did respectfully point out that I am *much older* than she and that the new space should reflect her youthful

ABOVE Old-world clocks are a mainstay in the world of junk and a favorite of ours. A room just wouldn't be complete without one.

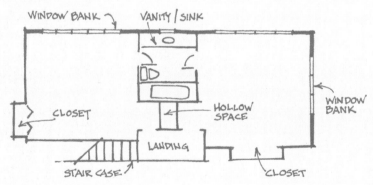

BEFORE

WINDOW BANK

VANITY / SINK

CLOSET

HOLLOW SPACE

WINDOW BANK

STAIR CASE

LANDING

CLOSET

AFTER

WINDOW BANK

BEDROOM

WALK IN CLOSET

OFFICE/ ACTIVITY ROOM

WORK STATION

DRESSING TABLE

WINDOW BANK

BALLET BAR & MIRROR

HALLWAY

STAIRCASE

VANITY SINK

SHOWER

STEPS

Barbara Milo Ohrbach   Antiqu

3 WISHES

Serene Slumber Room

Brand New Spa Bath

Creative Space

charm. After that conversation, I felt I was more in need of a face-lift than the room.

After much debate, we shook hands on a contemporary cottage look with industrial flair. This style would blend nicely with the existing interior decor and address E's need for a hip, hop, and happenin' space where she and her friends could kick back and chill. With that settled, it was time to put the plan into action.

LEFT To soften the hard lines of the industrial decor we added floral elements like this wildflower bloom.

BELOW For years we Whitneys have been collecting W's. This one stands on its own and works well as a bedside table or as a candleholder.

t Home

serene Slumber Room

Make it
p.197

BEFORE

KODAK E100VS

FACING PAGE A team of eclectic junk, including a glass light shade water fountain, helped to create this restful refuge.

FACING PAGE, INSET Even a nifty closet organizing system couldn't save our princess-in-training from classic clutter syndrome.

LEFT This is a clever and easy idea for a bedside reading lamp. Find an old ladder and clip on an industrial light from the garage.

BELOW A pillar candle takes its place atop a beautiful vintage mirror. The candle is wrapped with art paper to add the feminine touch.

This second floor space was originally a Jack and Jill space—two bedrooms with a bathroom in between. But the demands of high school brought need for a change. One room would remain a bedroom and the other would be designated for study and extracurricular activities.

GENERATIONS UNITE

Some things old and some things new joined forces to create a delightful place for quiet slumber. First, we painted over the green-striped walls with a gentle blue—far more conducive to a good night's rest. Ahh, parting is such sweet sorrow. Not!

Our new modern platform bed was lonely and needed some friends. The white crocheted bedspread from granny's attic was an excellent choice. The old ladder turned lamp and the car creeper at the foot of the bed for extra pillows rounded out our group of bedtime buddies.

Style Tweak

In its day this metal contraption held shirts—pressed, folded, and heavily starched—at a dry cleaner. We left it as is intentionally due to its industrial nature. To craft a cabinet with true cottage roots, spray paint it white and add beaded board over the wire shelving.

BELOW My teenaged gal pal is a hoarder of stuff. The metal shelving unit is just the thing to keep it contained and off the floor. I can dream, can't I?

Have you ever entered your teen's living quarters and instinctively run for cover because you didn't want to come face-to-face with the natural disaster you found the day before? Been there, done that. The answer lies in storage. The teen choice award for ultimate storage goes to large, open shelving units with plenty of space for all things preliberation.

MEANWHILE, BACK IN KANSAS

After the junk wizard fulfilled the wish for storage, it was back to the ranch for operation clutter clean up. Mess manage-ment for a teen is pretty basic after careful observation. A favorite of E's is casually dropping one item on each step as she ascends to her room.

If this sounds familiar, don't waste energy being angry because life's too short. Instead, break the routine by providing storage options that are as easy as the run-and-dump ritual. This metal dry cleaning rack is the perfect pitch-in and pull-out storage solution. It's so user-friendly that they can clean up with one hand, thus leaving the other free to send and receive important text messages.

ABOVE LEFT This rescue and reuse gets an A+. Pegboard salvaged from a warehouse is an imaginative disguise for popcorn ceilings.

ABOVE RIGHT A restaurant coatrack without its base was flipped upside down and topped with glass for an uncanny bedside table. Ingenious pegboard shoe molding matches the ceiling.

JUNKFO:
You can find aluminum molds, aka trinket holders, at almost any antique store for a good price. And if you don't need a holder for your trinkets, use one as a condiment server at your next dinner party.

Every person has a set of his or her own personal pet peeves. In our home, public enemy number one is the bifold door. It was time now to bid this set farewell. Fortunately, a makeup vanity was on the wish list. Because we added a walk-in closet, this one was a prime candidate for repurposing.

Old doors have a hundred and one uses. Here, the amalgamation of a white, weathered door, hollow threaded pipe, and flanges produced an inexpensive yet stylish makeup counter. We chose to leave the chipped paint on for junk authenticity. After sanding off the loose flakes, we applied a coat of polyurethane to encapsulate the lead paint. A very cool circa 1940s free-standing trifold mirror completes our cosmetic closet. Several vintage containers adorn the vanity to hold girlie necessities.

Who needs a gym when you can work your abs on the job for free? Stop, drop, and drill!

LEFT This former closet is now ready for a different kind of makeover, the teen-aged girl variety.

RIGHT Papier-mâché mannequin heads display the latest trend in UVB protection. They also remind E that big mother is always watching.

JUNKER'S
JUJU

Transform a bedroom from Bohemian gone bad into a stylish cottage industrial retreat fit for a princess with soft paint colors, cool metal junk, and earth-friendly cork floors.

1. PAINTS

A tranquil atmosphere with ethereal qualities was the vision for this space. Color selection was of utmost importance. The color medley is made up of three dreamy shades by Devine®. The bedroom and bathroom walls are a delicate shade of blue, Devine "Reflection." The bathroom ceiling, closet, and vanity walls are painted a subtle green, Devine "Blade." The hallway is a fresh and lively green, Devine "Gecko."

2. AND 3. STUFF

An unexpected combination of plastic and metal letters, pipe, glass globes, cottage textiles, cork, and dark woods come together to create a style we call "cottage industrial."

4. FABRICS

The white crocheted bedcover is complemented by bold pillows. The office chair cushions are covered with a blueish gray embroidered fabric that blends well with pastel Liberty prints and the drapery sheers.

③

Tweedle de and tweedle dum hard at work.

④

Brand New Spa Bath

A new cutting board, hardware store brackets, and vintage hooks team up as a clever wall shelf for a spa bath.

LEFT Unexpected accessory pieces like this small oilcan with a crystal suspended from the spout is what junking is all about.

RIGHT A quirky space allowed for some fun. Don't you think every girl should have a throne of her own?

The chance to build a brand new bathroom came as a surprise and was a perfect storm of opportunity. Framing found in the garage, a hollow wall at the top of the staircase, and excess closet space not only made it possible, but affordable. The space available was a little quirky, but that's what makes design interesting. After the plan was in place, it was time to pull out the sledgehammers and tear down some walls. There's nothing quite like demolition duty to release a little tension.

A bathroom should be crisp and clean. Many, including veteran junkers, may think that the bath is no place for junk. On the contrary! What could be more sanitary than a gurney from a hospital? The vanity, believe it or not, is such a retooled patient transporter. We removed one end, painted the whole thing white, and added a glass shelf below. Exposed pipes, conduit, and electrical boxes were partnered with the gurney to define this eclectic style.

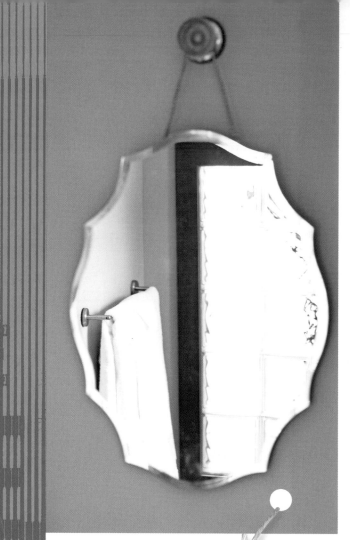

The reclaimed wood floors were one of our preeminent pickups. We got a lead on a house that was being remodeled and all of the wood ceilings were headed for the burn pile. Not a good thing. We rescued it and used much of it in projects throughout this book. What we couldn't use was donated to others.

What is the most comical castoff creation in this space? The door to the bathroom was found in our garage. When we moved into our home, I immediately dismantled the outdoor dog kennel, but couldn't bring myself to throw it away. Under protest from E, the door from the kennel was installed as her bathroom door. Recycling, it's a beautiful thing.

FACING PAGE An industrial hospital gurney turned vanity can put on a feminine face when adorned with accessories that possess girlish charm.

BELOW Lend the essence of tranquility to your bathroom with candles held by a discarded glass block.

JUNKFO:

There are stores that feature architectural hardware. In mint condition, hardware will cost you a chunk of change. Most of these stores have sections where they sell broken or imperfect pieces at discounted rates.

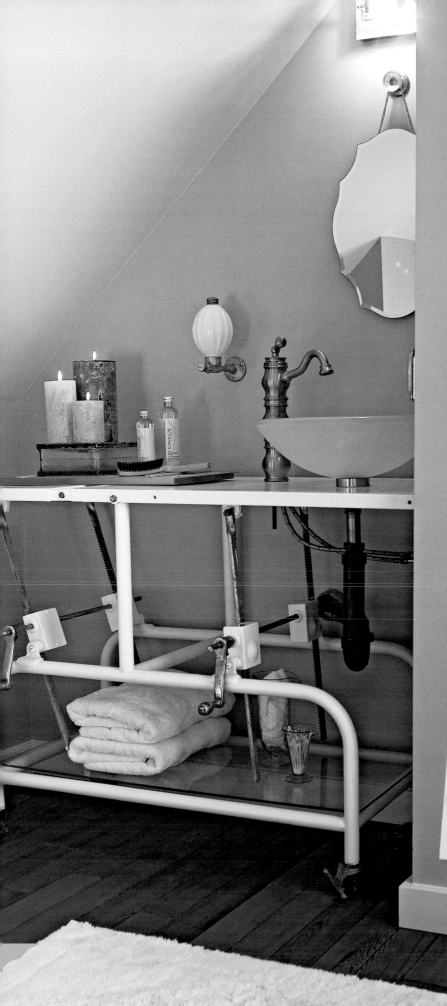

Cool, Mom pulled a Tom Sawyer on me.
She's good!

BELOW A glass block window was installed to make the room seem larger.

TOP RIGHT Curtain rings with a thing for bling hold the shower curtain designed from none other than recycled packing material.

BOTTOM RIGHT A two buck chuck shower curtain liner is attired in well-traveled bubble wrap and duct tape.

Sweet Details

1. **A MYSTERIOUS PEARL** and safety pin shade adorns a bathroom light fixture.

2. **GLASS BOTTLE STOPPERS** in gorgeous green are a delightful complement for a spa bath.

3. **ARE YOU CHARMED BY INK-WELLS?** Put your collection to work in the office to hold the small stuff on the desk.

4. **A LOVELY GLASS DISPLAY BOX** with a missing top makes it a bargain and an ideal makeup caddy.

5. **JUNK IS UNPREDICTABLE.** Without warning, we put crystals on a modish lampshade.

6. **THE HANDRAIL** standing in as a ballet bar is finished with a vintage glass doorknob.

Simplicity is the key to serenity. With that in mind the shower and its surrounding area were kept pure and simple. The bathroom is situated in an interior space with no option for a window to the great outdoors. A little sleight of hand and some recycled glass block created the illusion of a window in the shower wall.

The shower itself is your standard three by three with a kicker. But nothing is standard when one of the walls is a kneewall. Bright white wall tiles were installed for an open and airy feel, pebble floors for texture, and a wacky winding, exposed copper piping shower system to accommodate the kneewall.

Creative Space

You are now entering the final act of the suite makeover. With the sleeping quarters put to bed, the closet issues hung up, and the bathroom design completed, it's time to address the room of many faces. Miss E desired a room that could perform a multitude of tasks. As a high school student, she had to have a study studio. Her dream of becoming a fashion designer required an imagination station. And last, but not least, the girl was born for Broadway.

PERFORMANCE PLUS

These performance requests called for innovative thinking. Your typical desk would never do in this room. A trip to the hardware store provided a white laminate work surface that was installed from wall to wall. One half of the desktop was designated solely to E's fashion-forward goals, the other to book smarts.

LEFT Creativity can flow freely in a wide-open space equipped with all the right junk tools.

RIGHT Three very different types of junk come together as one very funky desk lamp. This is one for the record books.

Next it was time to address her dreams to one day see her name in lights on Broadway. A large mirror was affixed to the wall and a leftover handrail was converted to a ballet bar. Cork floors were installed to help cushion the blow, both on her legs and my ears below.

Whoa, Nellie! We're way ahead of the learning curve with this study station. That, of course, was the objective. Experience has taught us that student success is, at least in part, due to their surroundings. A clean and tidy spot with plenty of room to spread out is essential. This particular corner of the room was chosen due to the natural light streaming in on two sides. The more light the better when focusing on their face page. Oops, meant to say their history report.

To keep things in order, junk containers were called to task. Physician notebooks as bookshelves, inkwells to hold paper clips and rubber bands and an electrical fuse box paper holder are all members of the study group. A collection of vintage glass globes perched on the window ledge reflects the natural sunlight and offers inspiration when suffering from writer's block. As for the egg chairs, they are way too cool for school.

RIGHT The age of modern medicine supplied us with outmoded metal physician notebook covers to operate as bookshelves.

BELOW Here's a shocker. An industrial fuse box fitted with mason jars functions well as a paper and pencil container.

FAR LEFT Our teen's homework head-quarters is kept spit-spot and running smoothly with just a few junk organizers.

ABOVE This is what we refer to as dumb luck. We happened upon this "Whit-ney's" water bottle and without hesita-tion coughed up the dough.

LEFT Three industrial legs plucked from an abandoned ware-house hold up the white laminate work surface.

HOW TO:
Boot Form Lamp

MATERIALS NEEDED
- Vintage boot form
- Lamp shade of choice
- Crystals
- Lamp wiring kit (Note: Purchase lamp wiring kits at major hardware stores or visit www.grandbrass.com.)
- Threaded metal rod
- Lightbulb

TOOLS NEEDED
- Junker's Toolkit (see page 185)
- Wire stripper or utility knife

METHOD
1. Drill hole large enough for electrical cord at heel of boot form **A**.
2. Cut threaded rod to desired length.
3. Insert threaded rod through hole and attach strain relief, (aka the little black nut that relieves the tension on the wiring).
4. Thread electrical cord through hole at heel and out pre-existing hole and rod at top of boot with a wire coat hanger **B**.
5. Attach base of socket to rod and follow detailed wiring instructions included in lamp kit **C**.
6. Wire crystals on to lampshade with lightweight wire. Ours had pre-existing holes. If yours does not, measure and punch holes at equal intervals with a small paper punch **D**.

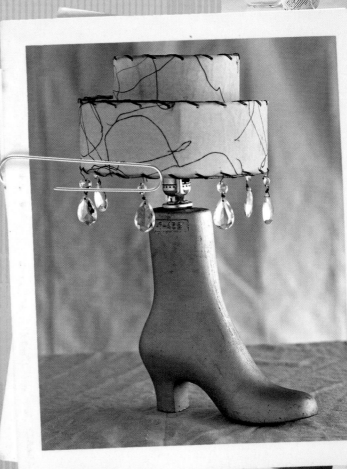

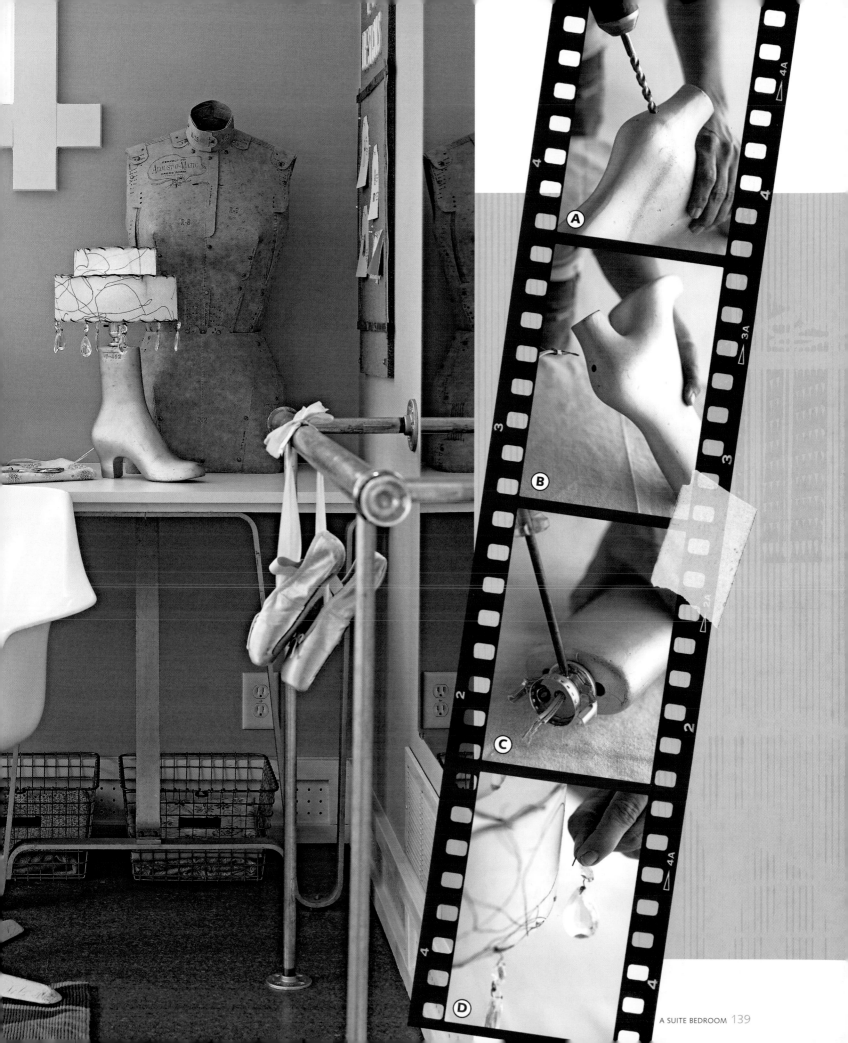

BELOW A corkboard makes friends with a collapsible metal ruler. The pair is the platform for style in the making.

RIGHT You may find balls of string a funny thing to buy, but they are awesome and actually quite useful.

FACING PAGE, BOTTOM After stretching at the barre, an aspiring ballerina can freshen up in the bathroom (at right).

E'S DESIGNS

Make it p.198

As you may suspect, the creative corner was a favorite project. E's true passion for the arts and her unbridled pursuit of excellence makes a right-brained mom stand up and take notice, not to mention overwhelmingly proud. Her design head-quarters deserved the same attention as its study partner down the hall.

A cardboard dress form in mint condi-tion was the catalyst for this creative crew of designer junk. An embroidery hoop encircling a dress drawing from a vintage art book, pincushions fashioned from string balls, and a presentation board crafted from new cork and old odds and ends were stitched together to make one girl's dream come true.

From time to time E needs to take a break from designing her next runway collection. Dancing is a great way to shake off the cobwebs, so to help her stay on pointe she can now head for the ballet bar without leaving home. A reconstructed handrail, dressed up with crystal doorknobs and mounted to the wall, is ideal for perfecting ballet basic positions. The wall mirror reflects her classical positions as well as her funkier hip-hop dance moves.

JUNKFO: Search out junk that speaks to your child's passion and you will show her the true beauty of recycling. Aspiring young designers flip for old dress forms and embroidery hoops.

EXECUTIVE HOME OFFICE

THE BROOKMANS
....

TWO MEN, A
LADY, AND A
DOG NAMED
CASEY

A STUDIOUS
CREW

RANCH, CIRCA
1980
....

Is working nine to five a way of life for you? Does school really end with the final bell of the day? Are scholastic days brought to a close upon receipt of a high school diploma? Most likely not, but dreaming never hurt anyone so keep it up. In the meantime, a well-appointed place to persevere at home will see you through until that mythical ship comes in. Our family of three, a professional mom, a soon to be high school whiz kid, and a young man at large on a college campus needed a shared space to burn the midnight oil. A family that works together stays together!

The first request from our family of deskmates was to be expected: organization. The office, more than any other room in the house, needs to be clutter-free and function-friendly. Otherwise, more time than necessary will be spent here searching for illusive ink cartridges and our happy homeowners will eat up too many precious hours. Like most families, our crew members have active school, work, and social calendars leaving little to no time to waste, so we needed to devise a plan that accommodated their demanding schedules. The closet was just the space we were looking for to begin this makeover. A closet credenza is a solid solution

2 WISHES

Family Work Post
Chess Corner

LEFT A cemetery row marker makes an excellent bookend. This may seem a little creepy, but it's still cool.

RIGHT Make your credenza function flawlessly with the help of junk containers.

FACING PAGE, INSET Bonus rooms don't have to be built over your garage. They can be found ready for revamp in your lower level.

to your workplace woes. It can accommodate just about everything your office demands, leaving the desk surface free of stuff and in high performance condition.

A CLOSET CAPER

The closet in this space, a longtime family employee, was deserving of a promotion. The doors were removed along with the shelving to make way for the credenza, a reformed rustic workbench. We believe that if you can see it, you can find it, so open storage was a principal element in our overall strategy. To that end, a gang of junkables were called to the task as a collaborative office supplies classification crew.

Family Work Post

Desk duty is a snap when office necessities are corralled close at hand on the credenza instead of the desktop.

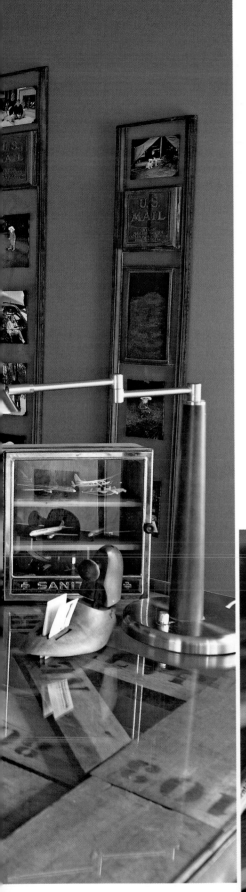

Ah yes, fresh off a long day at work and school and it's right back at it. Oh well, if there is work to be done, it may as well be done right. Unfortunately, our homeowners found themselves caught in a style power struggle. They adored their soft contemporary surroundings, but also enjoyed the character and charm that the oldies but goodies deliver. As angel investors of the junk world, we were there to help.

A NONHOSTILE MAKEOVER

OK, we're busted. Everything in the room got the cleaver, even the popcorn ceilings. Some things just have nothing to offer. All the furniture, though, was reassigned throughout the house. For the founder's new desk, a pallet exhibiting strong leadership qualities made for a perfect hire. The farmer's workbench as

ABOVE These days, the coffee is kept hot in a more contemporary fashion, leaving this old-time glass warmer to the pencils.

LEFT Our young male residents are fascinated with airplanes, cars, and travel. An airplane hanger of miniature proportions is crafted from an institutional sanitary cabinet.

a credenza added strong HR capabilities. The support staff now includes a store display rack for notebooks, industrial soap dispensers for supplies, and U.S. mail chutes to exhibit photos from the parties. How's that for a day at the office?

FOLLOW YOUR HEART

To enrich your office environment, look to your passions and aspirations for guidance. You will find this to be very helpful when searching for both old and new furniture and accessory pieces. The thoughtful combination in our space is a good example of this shopping strategy.

LEFT Occasionally, we throw a piece of junk into the mix as a novelty item. This old stapler was too good to pass up.

FACING PAGE A hymnal holder from the back of a church pew now holds magazines. We call that divine inspiration.

JUNKFO: Going-out-of-business sales can yield some pretty awesome junk. Look out for old hotels shutting down or being remodeled—you just may uncover a treasure like an old U.S. mail chute.

Our family wanted a contemporary look, but was wary of the room becoming too sterile. Intermingling well-worn woods found in the desktop and credenza, sleek metal objects like the mail chutes, and a new leather chair provided the best of both worlds.

Remember, a home office does not need to reflect the austere, depersonalized surroundings of your downtown cubicle. In fact, it should be quite the opposite. So go ahead and have some decorating fun. Personal touches like family photos and favorite collections are all welcome in a home-based workplace.

After finishing her juice box, Sue had time to play.

Yes, work does need to be done in an office. That doesn't mean the space has to be dull. The modern style of this office is enhanced by vibrant wall colors, rich leather furniture, and a contemporary collection of junk.

1. PAINTS

We were delighted to try out Aura® Paint, a new, environmentally friendly product from Benjamin Moore, which went on like butter. The Affinity color selection designed for Aura Paint is amazing. The rich colors we chose for the office were Montpelier (blue), Anjou Pear (green), Salsa Dancing (terra-cotta), and Metropolitan Gray on the ceiling.

2. FABRICS AND FLOORING

The beautiful terra-cotta leather chairs and coordinating pillows were purchased at Pier 1SM. The floor is bamboo, an earth-friendly product purchased from Lumber Liquidators. It looks like a million bucks, but it was very reasonably priced.

3. STUFF

Our junk focus in this room was mainly on the metal to provide the look and feel of modern design. The wood desk and credenza offered some relief from the hard metal pieces.

JUNKER'S JUJU

1   2   3

Fashion-forward pants, compliments of sheetrock dust.

Chess Corner

ABOVE Contemporary style should be spare, not stiff. The leather chairs add comfort to this seating ensemble.

FACING PAGE, LEFT One word: Awesome! A pair of nifty rear-view mirrors is attached to our incubator table as drink holders.

FACING PAGE, RIGHT We used big sheets of metal mesh that we found at a salvage yard. Our welder cut and banded them, and up they went.

Break time, JUNKMARKET style.

All work and no play makes for very dull junkers. To make their desk jobs more palatable, our homeowners wanted a place to engage in one of their favorite pastimes—playing a good game of chess and enjoying a cold beverage to sharpen their minds. Our table is quite the concoction crafted from an old incubator, metal pipes, and rearview mirrors.

The metal grate pieces helped get our juices flowing on this side of the room. They are oh so nice for displaying artwork. They also have magnetic personalities so they can be used as memo boards, to boot.

The younger gentleman of the house brought us a fabulous gift from his bedroom—the funky vintage floor lamp. A handsome, smart young man with good taste—what more could you ask for?

As for flooring, carpet may be nice on the toes but was not a good choice here. We selected bamboo, a renewable resource, to achieve the sleek look and help save the planet.

Sweet Details

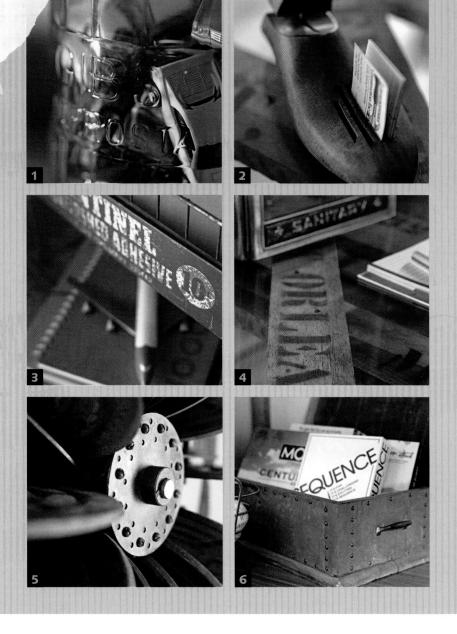

1. **TUPPERWARE®** took the place of glass storage jars in the refrigerator, leaving beauties like this available for small collection storage.

2. **A SHOE STRETCHER** is restored and ready to get to work as a business card holder.

3. **A METAL DISPLAY RACK** in the perfect shade of blue is just right for holding notebooks.

4. **THIS PALLET** is anything but average. It needed to see the world before retiring to a desk job.

5. **A RECORD EXCHANGER** emerged from the inside of a jukebox as a wonderful wall hanging.

6. **AN OLD METAL TRUNK** with wood casing is great for game storage.

This two-part office (one-part work, one-part fun) was designed to be sleek and open, which presented some storage predicaments. An office needs to be compartmentalized so small items like pens, pencils, and paper clips can be easily retrieved. Storage units for paper, notebooks, and games also need to be addressed.

SECRETS OF STORAGE

Office smalls are neatly displayed and contained in some smart ways. The industrial soap dispenser is categorically our favorite container. It holds the paper clips, the scissors, the pencils, and more. What's really cool? They come with keys and make surprisingly good secret safe deposit boxes. The metal store display

Make it
p.199

← Style Tweak

We know you have seen versions of this gadget holding nails in a workshop or maybe spices in the kitchen, but our streamlined metal soap dispenser flaunts a thoroughly modern style. To give it a traditional flair, employ a long, narrow old drawer instead of the dispenser and use more intricate lidded jars.

HOW TO:
Baguette-Baker Blinds

(A)

(B)

(C)

These baguette bakers—yes, for baking baguettes—were purchased from an import dealer at a flea market and are a very special find indeed. Granted, it takes an eye for junk to see window treatments in a contraption that flips loaves of bread. If you can't find the European variety, try looking in a used restaurant supply store.

MATERIALS NEEDED

- Baguette baking rack
- Hollow threaded pipe
- 4 flange connecters (Note: Choose ones about the same width as your baking rack is deep. Ours were 4 in. wide.)
- Skidmore's Wood Cleaner

TOOLS NEEDED

- Junker's Toolbox (see page 185)

METHOD

1. Remove linen covers from metal baguette holder (A).
2. Clean and brighten wood with Skidmore's Wood Cleaner (B).
3. Attach 2 round flange connectors to top of baguette baker (C).
4. Cut pieces of threaded pipe long enough for your baker to fit snugly in the window opening.
5. Thread pipe into flanges attached to baguette maker.
6. Attach 2 remaining flanges to top of both pieces of pipe.
7. Slide into window opening. Sized correctly it will be secure without screws.

rack is another of our pet pieces. It's a great storage device and looks good, too.

One reason we chose this space was to prove once and for all that basement areas can be just as beautiful.

CLEVER COVER-UPS

Fortunately, the space was blessed with a large window allowing for natural sunlight to shine in, creating an inviting atmosphere. The scenery outside the generous window was not as picturesque as a main floor view. And there was the inevitable and unsightly fuse box. Lucky for us, our issues were easily solved, or should we say concealed? The window was dressed with baguette bakers that seemed to be tailor-made. The fuse box was disguised with corkboard and finished off with metal strapping and refrigerator hinges.

LEFT Break the eye level rule when hanging artwork. Black and whites hung low add intrigue to your room.

BELOW These hip baguette bakers are natural-born window blinds. The lever to release the bread is a built-in opening and closing device.

I almost work better if I don't

Write the great american novel
Tell the President
invent better wheel
finish paper for english

Chapter 4 Final Review

1. Find the values of x, y, and z

JUNKFO:
Check out a swap meet for items like strapping tape and hinges. Swap meet vendors, unlike flea market vendors, focus more on $2 to $10 items for the "true" value seeker.

SPA AMONG THE CEDARS

THE RENARDS

....

EMPTY NESTERS
WITH A GOOD-
LOOKING
GOLDEN

DESPERATELY
SEEKING SPA
TREATMENTS

LAKESIDE RETREAT,
CIRCA 1984

....

When it comes to redoing your bathroom, for heaven's sake don't flush away your creativity like a departed goldfish. Although many of you may think of a bathroom as one of the more utilitarian spaces in your home, we view them as more of a sanctuary. After all, why should you skimp on the one place where you can truly be alone with your thoughts?

The old bath, wicked nice in the 1980s, was long overdue for a make-over. Our guiding light for design came from the woodsy, lakeside setting of the home. The natural "campy" decor we chose befitted a cozy cabin by the lake. Now that's what we call keeping it real!

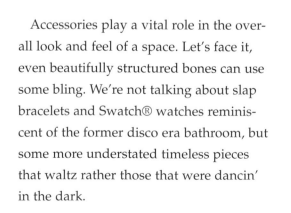

4 WISHES

Soaking Tub

Crafty Cupboard

Sink in Style

Privacy Nook

Accessories play a vital role in the overall look and feel of a space. Let's face it, even beautifully structured bones can use some bling. We're not talking about slap bracelets and Swatch® watches reminiscent of the former disco era bathroom, but some more understated timeless pieces that waltz rather those that were dancin' in the dark.

Not only should each junk accessory be selected with care, but you should be mindful of the overall composition; you know, that pretty picture you have painted in your head. We recommend a combination of texture and materials that will produce the eye candy factor. Our Brach's® bag includes a fabric and metal stool, a wooden grain scoop, and a metal industrial gauge.

BEFORE

FACING PAGE, LEFT
A reclaimed, hand-
made stool crafted
from bottle caps and
vintage hooks for
legs. All we needed
to do was reupholster
it. Sometimes you
just get lucky.

FACING PAGE,
RIGHT Here's some
gauge advice. If you
come across one, buy
it. We love stuff that
can be recycled from
room to room, and
gauges fit the bill.

LEFT Getting the lat-
est scoop from your
magazines is easy
when kept close at
hand. Corral your
reading material in
an unemployed grain
scoop.

ABOVE Replacing an
oversized platform
tub with the claw-
foot variety will save
space and provide a
splash of elegance.

Soaking Tub

S plish, splash, who wouldn't want to take a bath in a room that radiates rustic elegance? We all agree, after hitting it hard through the course of a day, it sure feels good to get away from it all. If you're in the market for a bathroom renovation, try this woodsy redo on for size. It may appear a bit indulgent for a junker, but never fear, these are budget-friendly bubbles. It's all true, you can have style without emptying your piggy bank.

JUNK BY DESIGN

"Where to begin?" is one of the most frequently asked questions we hear when designing with junk. Start by choosing one piece that offers creative influence for the space. Our target was to fashion an indoor room that embraced the spirit of the great outdoors, hence the bath caddy crafted from a birch tree trunk. When this idea was hatched, more than a few eyebrows were raised. Of course, those reservations only spurred us on more. Remember, a little ingenuity can take you a long way. Catch you on the next page— Calgon™ and candles are calling!

shopping for tubs in a parking lot is the latest craze. Try it sometime!

Make it
p. 201

An auger is far from boring when used to display family camp photos. A welder was called in to affix metal hanging mounts to it before it was screwed to studs in the wall.

FACING PAGE, LEFT Hardworking oval snowshoes take a step inside to hold candles and bath basics. They adapted nicely to the steamy surroundings.

FACING PAGE, RIGHT This auger embodies the perfect balance of rugged construction and a delicately turned line.

While soaking in the great indoors, you'll have free time to enjoy some memories from days gone by. Photos authenticating family fish tales are tailor-made additions to our lodgelike atmosphere.

DISPLAY JUNK

An idle auger is back in the saddle as a display rod. Wrap your impeccable sense of style around this artful concept. Purchase some inexpensive frames (old or new), place some playful black-and-whites inside, and suspend from the auger with leather cord purchased at your local craft store. No vintage pictures of your own kin? Pick some up at a flea market. Who's going to challenge you, Mr. Bubble®?

Speaking of Mr. B., we wanted our bath hardware set up to run water and produce bubbles in a style that complemented the campy decor. We purchased an old-world reproduction unit that included a shiny faucet, separate hot and cold handles, and a handheld shower. Our second-hand tub was lacking holes for hardware, so we solved the problem by floor mounting the bath fixtures on industrial exposed pipes. The steel pipes used here blended nicely with the metal brackets we employed to hang the barn board walls.

Sorry to burst your bath bubbles, but eventually, like it or not, you will have to remove yourself from the tub. Maybe the water has gone cold or reality is beckoning. Either way, you'll need a fluffy towel to make the transition a little less painful. Keep a stack within reach on a shelf styled from a perfectly painted shutter.

When we came across this shutter, we instinctively knew it was the perfect piece of junk for what we had in mind. Towels are a necessity that can also be used as a decorative accent in the bathroom. So why hide them in the cupboard? Open storage is both charming and user friendly. One glance will tell you that you are out of towels, preventing that shivering cry for help to the outside world. As for those beautifully arranged towels on the bar, keep your mitts off those; Mom says they are for company only.

LEFT A hollow steel rod capped with metal furniture sliders holds the revered guest towels. A pair of antlers (why not?) secured to the wall with metal flanges supports the rod.

RIGHT Cool metal molds are a dime a dozen. Put them to use as a no-fuss, no-muss candle holder. Add candles and pebbles, then lie back and relax—your work here is done.

JUNKFO:

Cutting antlers is not risky business, but it is stinky business. Wear a mask, cut in a well-ventilated room, then run for your life. Your nose will thank you.

HOW TO:
A Mod Prayer Chair

Découpage is making a comeback. Use lightweight textiles instead of paper to beautify a beaten up old prayer chair.

MATERIALS NEEDED
• Lightweight quilting fabric
• Mod Podge® or other découpage sealer
• Upholstery tacks
• Grosgrain ribbon

TOOLS NEEDED
• Junker's Toolbox (see page 185)

METHOD
1. Lightly sand chair and prep to apply Mod Podge.
2. Cut fabric to cover chosen surfaces, allowing a small excess of fabric on each side Ⓐ.
3. Apply a layer of Mod Podge to wood and lay fabric on wet glue, making sure that it is smooth. Allow to dry for 30 minutes.
4. When dry, apply Mod Podge directly to the fabric allowing to dry again for 30 minutes. Repeat this step 3 to 5 times Ⓑ.
5. After the final coat of Modge Podge has been applied and is dry, spray fab-

ric with water, then sand while still wet for a smooth finish Ⓒ.
6. Remove excess fabric from edges with an X-Acto® knife.
7. Attach grosgrain ribbon where desired with fabric glue and secure with upholstery tacks.

Crafty Cupboard

Nobody wants to find themselves in a tight corner. To alleviate this room's shut-in feeling we said ta-ta to the economy-size built-ins and hi-de-ho to more space-appropriate freestanding elements. The vanity was the first to go, replaced by a pedestal sink. Next on the chopping block was the larger-than-life cabinet. Quick, somebody go get the chain saw! Storage is a crucial component in every commode, but there are better options.

THE SNAPPY CABINET

We love this Welch dresser. It's relatively small in scale, providing the sense of spaciousness so desperately needed, and gave us the necessary catchall storage. The piece has plenty of open shelving up top and space below with doors for all of those items that don't really need to be seen. And voilà, we accomplished what we set out to do with elbow room to spare.

FACING PAGE Consider replacing built-ins with elegant antique furniture pieces that simultaneously confer character and give you more room to groom.

ABOVE LEFT Plucked from Ricky Ricardo's recording studio, these tiny bongos may have been too small for his big Cuban sound but they're just right for cotton balls and swabs.

ABOVE RIGHT Here's one that didn't get away. We strung up a picture of our pint-size big-game hunter by adding a grommet for reinforcement and attaching it to a fish stringer.

Make it
p.200

Pop the corks on vintage bottles, add water, and some sweet smelling flowers for a lavish touch to a campy latrine.

RIGHT When accessorizing, hunt for castoffs that compliment the theme. A camp toaster, that's the ticket!

JUNKFO:

Remember, one person's junk can be a breath of fresh air to someone else. When remodeling don't pitch it; pitch in. Used cabinetry, toilets, and sinks can all be donated to your local building reuse center.

Establishing proper proportions in a room is only half the battle. After you are satisfied with the framework and placement of the focal pieces, it's time to play dress up. First things first. The silk floral arrangement was bid a long overdue farewell and replaced with some junky-dory accents. A word of caution, accessory pieces are meant to add ambiance, not clutter. When decorating, ask yourself this question: At the end of the day, do I want my room to look more like Audrey Hepburn or Cindy Lauper? We hope you agree that the little black dress with pearls is the obvious choice.

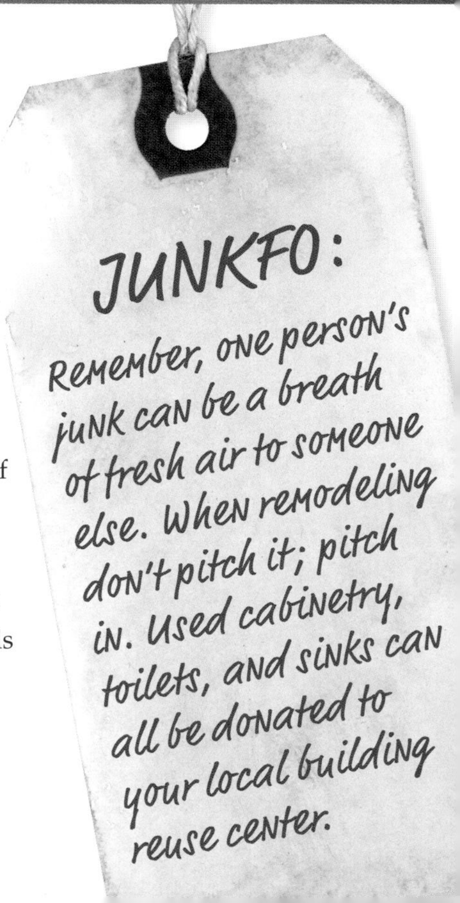

①

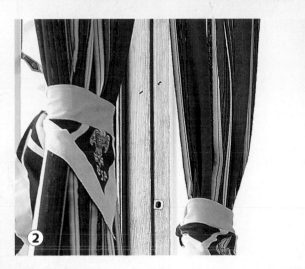

②

JUNKER'S JUJU

Bold and sassy Adirondack colors were what our camp counselors wanted. Our initial color cue was taken from the perfectly weathered barn board we had chosen for the walls. But when we found the rug, the room sprung to life. The rest just flowed off the tips of our fingers.

1. PAINT

Our paint selection for the walls was Ale by Devine. The lighter wall stripes and ceiling color were developed on sight by mixing equal parts of Ale and white.

2. FABRIC

The window treatments in this lovely loo were fashioned from a store-bought Waverly® drapery panel. This is a less expensive alternative than starting from scratch.

3. STUFF

We wanted the junkables to reflect the feeling of being tucked inside a cabin on a snowy Saturday. Snowshoes and game pieces reminded us of north woods family vacations.

③

Sink in Style

The term hodgepodge is music to a junker's ear. If this room were a Hollywood hit, the sink setup would win an Oscar for best original score. Think about it, in the beginning of the musical *Dirty Dancing*, "Baby" Houseman and bad boy Johnny Castle were far more likely to exchange blows than to form the bond of everlasting friendship.

JUNKOLOGIES

Like people, roadside rejects have different personalities, but that doesn't mean they can't establish the ties that bind. Our junk came from all different walks of life. With some thoughtful composition, an ancient tin mirror and metal frying basket can indeed live together in harmony.

An old suitcase, a pressed tin mirror frame and a revived prayer chair make for a bona fide collection of odd yet stunning attire for a north woods retreat.

ABOVE LEFT Our soap dish, a fancy piece of junk from the Victorian era combined with a contemporary bowl, is a touch of unexpected elegance in our lakeside loo.

FACING PAGE, INSET Pity the woman who has to do her makeup under lighting that looks more like a bug zapper.

Mixing is an art form, so take your time when orchestrating your masterpiece. If you do, together your junk will be some kind of wonderful.

Another form of mixing shows up on the handsome walls in this bathroom. Barn board wall coverings play an important role here, but were too heavy to cover them all. To change it up a bit, we left the sink walls open for a contrasting technique. Big, bold, and beautiful stripes were our choice. The darker shade matches the color found on the walls above the rustic wainscot and the lighter stripes repeat the ceiling shade. The flat striped walls provided the perfect canvas for showcasing our eclectic junk ensemble.

BEFORE

KODAK E100VS   44   45

Bathrooms are 24/7 workaday spaces and need to be designed with practicality in mind. Don't let that stop you from throwing in a little form to go with all that function. A shot of clever design consideration, combined with some excellent refurbished rubbish will allow you to pull together a task-oriented space all wrapped up with a pretty bow. The fun of this design challenge is not only in the decorating phase but also in the hunt for junk. You can expect to be scouring places like used restaurant supply outlets, tag sales, and antique stores.

FUNKY FUNCTIONALITY

Fresh air is a beautiful thing, especially in a bathroom. Once the cumbersome vanity was demoed, we had a clean slate with which to work. Wow, now that *was* a breath of fresh air.

The inevitable "what to do?" time was then upon us. We decided "pristine with a dab of color" was the right way to go. Pristine came in the form of a shiny, bright, space-saving pedestal sink. The color? A fun, funky, and functional assortment of junk. A suitcase and a grain scoop? Some folks say, why? We say, go for it!

FACING PAGE, LEFT
Greet your guests
with a message in the
soap dish. As you can
see, we need some
lessons in Boggle®.

FACING PAGE,
RIGHT Sometimes
it's just about getting
a smile. A folk art
doggy will wag
its tail under any
circumstance.

Style Tweak

A retired restaurant frying basket is right at home holding hand towels in the warm and toasty surrounds of a bath-room. But if a commercial restaurant gadget doesn't appeal, try using a small wooden drawer with decorative carving for a softer, more traditional sense of style.

Privacy Nook

TO LET

Let your whimsical self out of the bag when decorating with junk. Boy Scout scarves, horse bridles, and hibachi grills? Hard to believe, but they really do play well together.

Nature calls! If you have a job to do, you may as well have fun with it. Take a look at the great finish details in this privacy nook. At first glance they may appear pretty traditional, but upon closer inspection you will discover that they are a little zanier than you first thought. Weathered boards, salvaged from an about to be bulldozed barn were an innovative choice for covering the cold concrete walls. The barn board provided the warm, cozy feel that this space was missing.

We attached the board with industrial glue and concrete nails, then screwed on angle iron at the top and bottom edges for a sure finish. Again, an out-of-the-box combo of junk frills were carefully selected and placed to finish the job. Using junk in whacky ways is fun and will inevitably produce an uncannily good end result.

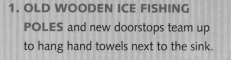

sweet Details

1. **OLD WOODEN ICE FISHING POLES** and new doorstops team up to hang hand towels next to the sink.

2. **SAVE YOUR BOTTLE CAPS**, kids. They adorn a stool here, but think frames, too.

3. **SHORT PIECES** of one-of-a-kind moldings are easy to find and great for small projects with big impact.

4. **AN ORNATE VICTORIAN IRON PIECE** with the addition of a contemporary bowl becomes a hand-soap caddy.

5. **PRESSED CEILING TIN** is tried-and-true junk. A frame for a bathroom mirror is just one of many ways to use this fabulous material.

6. **A BRIDLE** turned toilet paper holder. No tools required.

As we often say, it's all in the details. This bathroom redo is a prime example of this design principle. After making a bold statement by selecting and utilizing a seemingly risky combination of barn-board walls with steel supports, inexpensive faux pebble linoleum tile, and freestanding antique furniture, the stage was set for creative fun with accessory pieces.

Our motto here was anything goes, keeping in mind that it's not about the match, it's about the mix. Farm fresh junk, chucked out cabin goodies, and salvaged folk art pieces may not strike you as likely decorative partners, but it's a feel good moment when you see them all together. So take this cue from us, and feel free to experiment.

Style Tweak

We used a game piece from a vintage ring toss set to hold back one of our plushy bath sheets. It's a great way to underscore the sporty theme of our campy retreat and get the job done, too. If crafty is more your thing, consider knotting a macramé tieback.

Our collection of junk needed to be on solid ground, so the flooring selection was of utmost importance. The floor tile in this room has its roots firmly established in a different era, but it is new and improved to meet today's standards. Yes, indeed, linoleum has returned in a big way. Our spa among the cedars needed a floor that was durable and fit our natural theme. Our pick was tile that has a black background with a realistic earthy colored pebble design. The colors of nature found in this flooring helped us to get the rest of this retreat well under foot.

HOW TO MAKE THE REST

DISCLAIMER: The junk used in our projects may be one-of-a-kind items. The instructions on these pages refer only to how we transformed the junk we found. You may need to improvise to achieve desired transformation—and chances are, your stuff will look all the better!

Junker's Toolbox:

- Drill
- Assorted drill bits for metal and wood
- Screwdriver
- Hammer
- Wood saw
- Miter saw

- Metal saw
- Pliers (straight and needlenose)
- Tape measure
- Straightedge
- Marker
- Bolt cutter

- Heavy wire cutter
- Pry bar
- Paint brushes
- Sanding blocks or paper

p. 19

Bird Cage Light Fixture

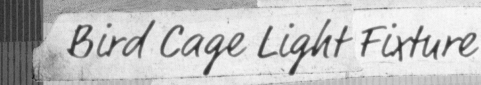

MATERIALS

- Old birdcage
- SVT cord
- Plug
- Strain relief
- Threaded metal rod, ⅛ IP
- Antique finish socket
- Crystal clear decorative round lightbulb
- Nut

TOOLS

- Junker's Toolbox
- Wire stripper or utility knife

METHOD

1. Remove top hanger of birdcage (if necessary) and drill hole larger to accommodate threaded rod **(A)**.

2. Cut metal rod to desired length (ours was 5 in.). Tip: Before cutting rod, screw the nut on after cutting off the rod screw—this will rethread any damaged metal.

3. Insert thread rod through hole, attach strain relief on top of cage, and secure from inside with nut **(B)**.

4. Attach base of socket to rod.

5. Insert SVT cord through strain relief, rod, and socket bottom, wire to the socket, and snap the socket together **(C)** (refer to your lighting supply company for wiring instructions).

6. Attach top of strain relief and tighten **(D)**.

7. Wire plug.

FORECAST

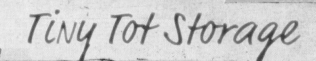

Tiny Tot Storage

MATERIALS
- 2 pieces of old molding or new 1 x 4 boards
- 6 vintage cast-iron brackets or new brackets
- 3 potato crates
- 3 covered storage baskets

TOOLS
- Junker's Toolbox
- Skidmore's Wood Finish

METHOD

1. Measure and cut molding or new boards (ours were each 6 ft. in length). If you're using new boards, finish as desired **Ⓐ**.

2. Screw boards to wall using screw anchors. Boards should be approximately 24 in. apart to accommodate potato crates.

3. Measure and attach brackets (ours are 12 in. deep) in pairs to molding, making sure they are level. Allow enough space between each set to accommodate storage baskets **Ⓑ**.

4. Finish potato crates with Skidmore's Wood Finish and set on brackets **Ⓒ**.

5. Set covered storage baskets inside potato crates. (Our baskets are 20 x 15 x 10.)

p. 20

SHIPSHAPE

Caster Easel

MATERIALS
- 2 vintage matching casters
- Scrap wood
- Screws
- Swelling wood glue

TOOLS
- Junker's Toolbox

METHOD

1. Cut 2 pieces of scrap wood (ours were 7½ x 1⅜ x ⅝).

2. Mark and drill holes for casters  (A) (ours were 5 in. apart). Tip: Caster shafts are usually cone shaped—drill partially through the top of the wood using a smaller bit, and drill through the bottom side using a larger bit. This will accommodate the variance in the shaft and allow a snug fit.

3. Screw vertical wood piece to horizontal piece so that the bottom of the vertical piece is even with the casters (B).

4. Insert caster shafts into holes and secure with wood swelling glue (C), (D). Note: Be sure to leave enough space between caster shafts and vertical wood piece to accommodate display item.

p. 33

(A)

(B)

(C)

(D)

SUPPER CLUB

Sewing Cabinet Hall Table

p. 44

MATERIALS

- Old sewing cabinet
- Old galvanized garden edging
- Vintage drawer pull
- Bolts/washers/nuts
- Hammered "metal" look paint
- Wood putty

TOOLS

- Junker's Toolbox

METHOD

1. Remove sewing machine and front door from cabinet **(A)**.

2. Wood putty holes and sand.

3. Lightly sand cabinet so paint will adhere.

4. Paint cabinet following instructions on paint label **(B)**.

5. Measure and cut garden edging with tin snips **(C)**.

6. Mark for bolts on garden edging and drill **(D)**.

7. Place edging on cabinet face and drill bolt holes in wood.

8. Insert bolts and secure with washers and nuts.

9. Attach decorative drawer pull.

(A)

(B)

(C)

(D)

p. 45

Metal Art Frames

MATERIALS
- Metal window frame
- Black matting board or 4 precut mat boards
- Lightweight and narrow double-stick Velcro
- Artist tape
- 2 small eye hooks
- Hanging wire

TOOLS
- Junker's Toolbox
- X-Acto knife or mat cutter
- Metal drill bit

METHOD

1. Measure openings on metal frame (we used metal, but you could use a wood frame).

2. Measure and cut mat board ½ to 1 in. larger than the frame opening on all 4 sides (trim precut mats as necessary).

3. Measure and cut the opening of the mat board (ours is 8 in. by 10 in.).

4. Measure and cut 8 strips of double-stick Velcro. One for the top and bottom of each mat.

5. Attach Velcro to the top and bottom of each opening on the frame.

6. Attach remaining Velcro to front top and bottom of mat boards.

7. Attach mat boards to frames with Velcro.

8. Measure and pre-drill holes for eye hooks on the top corners of the window frame.

9. Screw in eye hooks.

10. Measure, cut, and attach wire for hanging.

11. Attach artwork to mats using artist's tape. This will allow you to remove the drawing without damaging the paper.

DELECTABLE DINING

Stool-Top Bench

MATERIALS
- Wood 1 x 8's
- Wood 1 x 2's
- Screws
- Wood glue
- 2 old stool tops
- Wood finish

TOOLS
- Junker's Toolbox

METHOD
1. Measure and cut the 1 x 8's for the sides. Ours are at 4 ft. and 1 ft.

2. Measure and cut the 1 x 2's to appropriate length for 4 braces and the feet Ⓐ.

3. Glue and screw braces to inside corners leaving a 1-in. space between the boards.

4. Attach the feet Ⓑ.

5. Measure and cut blocks for stool seats the appropriate length.

6. Attach blocks to bottom of seat, fitting them snugly inside the sides of bench Ⓒ.

7. Finish as desired.

p. 50

LAUNDRY LOUNGE

Sewing Machine Thread Holder

MATERIALS
- Old hardware store small tool holder
- Screws
- Washers and nuts

TOOLS
- Junker's Toolbox

METHOD
1. Place a washer at top and bottom of existing holes in tool holder Ⓐ.

2. Insert screws and lock into position with nuts Ⓑ.

3. Remove bottom shelf to allow you to repeat process for that shelf.

4. Reattach bottom shelf to tool holder Ⓒ.

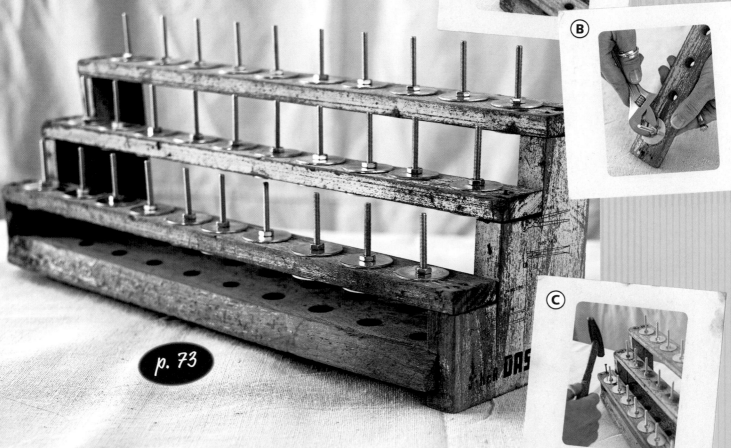

p. 73

MAKING AN ENTRANCE

p. 87

Boot Form Tray

MATERIALS
- Wooden boot stretcher/form
- Wood dowels or scraps
- Restaurant tray
- Wood finish
- Self-adhesive Velcro strips

TOOLS
- Junker's Toolbox

METHOD
1. Cut ends of boot stretcher at angle to work with the curve of the tray Ⓐ.

2. Measure, cut, and attach dowels or wood pieces to boot stretcher to keep tray level.

3. Apply wood finish Ⓑ.

4. Attach Velcro to wood with stapler gun and to tray with self-adhesive Ⓒ.

Ⓐ

Ⓒ

Ⓑ

Swedish Crate Shelf

MATERIALS
- Slotted crate
- Miscellaneous vintage hardware for keys, etc.
- Wood pieces for shelves and supports
- Screws/upholstery tacks
- Wood finish

TOOLS
- Junker's Toolbox
- Wood measuring strips

METHOD
1. The sides of our crate were angled, so to measure the angle, we loosely attached two strips of wood together and placed them inside of the crate to form an angle. Using this template, we were able to draw the board's angle on the shelf.

2. Measure and cut supports for sides Ⓐ.

3. Measure spacing and attach supports to crate.

4. Wood finish crate and shelves Ⓑ.

5. Attach hardware for keys, miscellaneous hardware, etc., with upholstery tacks or screws Ⓒ.

6. Insert shelves.

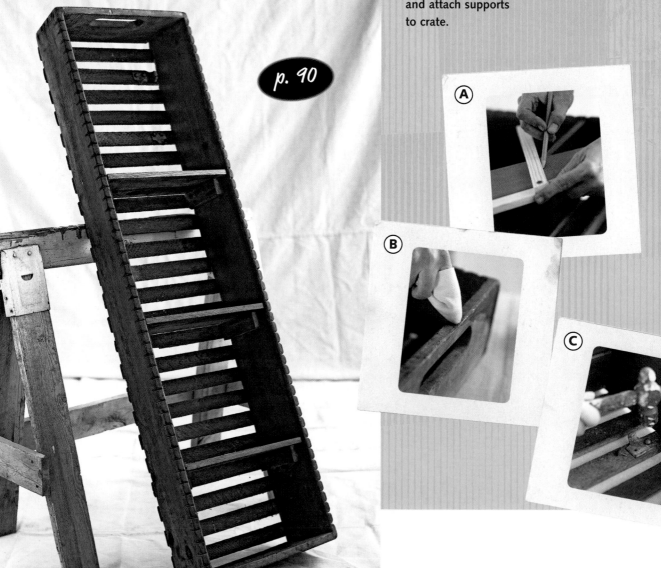

p. 90

p.114

A

B

C

Iron Gate Coffee Table

MATERIALS
- Piece of iron railing
- Scrap wood
- Screws
- 4 table legs
- 4 hinges (if desired)
- Surface protectors (clear)

TOOLS
- Junker's Toolbox

METHOD

1. Cut table legs to desired height (ours is 18 in.).

2. Attach legs to railing Ⓐ.

3. Measure and cut scrap boards to edge the outside of the railing (miter corners) Ⓑ.

4. Screw the cut boards to legs/railing Ⓒ.

5. Add decorative hinges on corners (if desired).

6. Measure (but have professionally cut) glass to fit.

7. Attach protectors to railing, insert glass.

Corbel Frame Holder

p. 105

MATERIALS

- Corbel (ours is 7 x 5 x 18)
- Scrap wood for base
- 2 matching vintage wire hooks
- Handles (if desired)
- Screws

TOOLS

- Junker's Toolbox

METHOD

1. Measure and cut scrap wood slightly larger than corbel Ⓐ.

2. Clip screw ends off wire hooks with bolt cutter.

3. Attach hooks to corbel as shown, making sure they are level to each other Ⓑ.

4. Attach base to the bottom of the corbel.

5. Add handles for legs if desired Ⓒ.

Ⓐ

Ⓑ

Ⓒ

A SUITE BEDROOM

Glass Lamp Shade Water Fountain

MATERIALS

- 2 glass ceiling lamp shades of similar size
- Glass adhesive
- Small submersible fountain pump with adjustable water flow
- ½ in. rubber hose
- Rocks

TOOLS

- Junker's Toolbox

METHOD

1. Glue lamp shades together at their tops. One becomes the base, the other the basin (A).

2. Cut hose the appropriate length. Ours is 1½ in. (B).

3. Slip hose over spout on pump.

4. Place pump in center of the lamp shade basin.

5. Slide a decorative piece of hardware to hide black hose if desired (C).

6. Add rocks to cover pump.

(A)

(B)

(C)

p. 120

Ruler Bulletin Board

MATERIALS

- Heavy-duty sheet of cork
- Bendable metal ruler
- Heavy-duty double-stick mounting tape
- Screws and nuts
- Plastic punch letters

TOOLS

- Junker's Toolbox

METHOD

1. Measure and cut cork to appropriate size.

2. Adhere one side of double-stick mounting tape to bendable ruler Ⓐ.

3. Bend ruler into box position Ⓑ.

4. Remove tape to adhere bendable ruler to cork.

5. Drill holes in each corner of cork.

6. Put nut over each hole and put screw in place Ⓒ.

7. Spell out your desired message with plastic letters.

E'S DESIGNS

p. 140

Ⓐ

Ⓑ

Ⓒ

EXECUTIVE HOME OFFICE

Soap Dispenser Office Supply Caddy

MATERIALS
- Industrial soap dispenser
- 5 baby food jars with metal lids
- 1 x 4 piece of lumber

TOOLS
- Junker's Toolbox

METHOD

1. Measure and mark bottom of soap dish for placement of baby food jars.

2. Predrill holes in bottom of soap dispenser Ⓐ.

3. Measure inside of soap dispenser and cut 1 x 4 to fit Ⓑ.

4. Slide 1 x 4 inside of soap dispenser Ⓒ.

5. Predrill holes in center of baby jar lids.

6. Place lids over predrilled holes on the bottom of soap dispenser and attach together with wood screws.

7. Screw baby food jars into lids.

p. 155

SPA AMONG THE

Camp Toaster Votive

p. 174

MATERIALS
- Zinc jar lid
- Camp toaster
- Bolt/wing nut

TOOLS
- Junker's Toolbox

METHOD
1. Carefully break glass inside zinc lid and remove (A).

2. Drill hole in base of toaster (B).

3. Drill hole in center of zinc lid.

4. Attach lid to toaster with bolt and nut (C).

5. Add votive.

CEDARS

A

B

C

shutter shelf

MATERIALS
- 1 wide shutter
- 2 shelf brackets
- Screws
- Polyurethane

TOOLS
- Junker's Toolbox

METHOD
1. Measure and cut bottom of shutter for shelf **A**.

2. Spray shutter pieces with poly-urethane to protect chippy finish **B**.

3. Attach shutter pieces with shelf brackets **C**.

p. 165

RESOURCES

ANNIE'S ATTIC
1205 Highway 25 N
Buffalo, MN 55313-1939
Phone: 763-682-2818

ARCHITECTURAL ANTIQUES
1330 Quincy Street NE
Minneapolis, MN 55413
612-332-8344

BENJAMIN MOORE PAINTS
www.benjaminmoore.com

**BUFFALO NICKEL
ANTIQUE MALL**
1004 S 3 Street
763-682-4735
www.buffalonickelantiques.com

CAM CONSTRUCTION
403 Whiskey Road NW
Isanti, MN 55404

**COST PLUS WORLD
MARKET**
www.worldmarket.com

CRATE AND BARRELSM
www.crateandbarrel.com

D'KORE WELDING
Delaney Construction
3435 County Road 92 N
Maple Plain, MN 55359
612-479-1296

DEVINE PAINTS
www.devinecolor.com

**FULLERTON LUMBER
COMPANY**
2860 Highway 25
Watertown, MN 55388
952-955-2237

GARDEN GATE FLOWERS
5023 France Ave S
Minneapolis, MN 55410
612-929-8030

**HIRSHFIELD'S DECORATING
CENTERS**
725 Second Avenue N
Minneapolis, MN 55405
612-377-3910
www.hirshfields.com

HUNT AND GATHER
4944 Xerxes Ave. South
Minneapolis, MN 55410
612-455-0250
www.huntandgatherantiques
.com

ID DESIGN
211 N 1st Street
Minneapolis, MN 55401
612-317-0045

IKEA®
www.ikea.com

JOANN FABRICSSM
www.joann.com

KELLEY & KELLEY NURSERY
2325 Watertown Rd
Long Lake, Minnesota 55356
952-473-7337

**LEMMERMAN
CONSTRUCTION, INC**
9037 Co Rd 17 S.E.
Delano, MN 55328
763-972-3003

LUMBER LIQUIDATORSSM
952-314-4975
www.lumberliquidators.com

MICHAELS®
www.michaels.com

OTTEN BROS.
2350 W. Wayzata Blvd.
Long Lake, MN, USA
952-473-5425

PIER 1
www.pier1.com

POTTERY BARN®
www.potterybarn.com

RPK CONSTRUCTION
221 Ash Avenue South
Mayer, MN 55360
612-618-0126

**SOLID CONCRETE
STUDIO INC.**
1200 Lincoln Ave.
St. Paul, MN 55105
651-707-2652

**SOMERS LAKE
CONSTRUCTION INC**
6631 80th Street NW
Maple Lake, MN 55358

SR HARRIS
8865 Zealand Ave N.
Brooklyn Park, MN 55445
763-424-3500
www.srharrisfabric.com

STEVE SANTANA PLUMBING
612-816-1619

TOWN HOME PAINTING
612-598-5615

TARGET®
www.target.com

**WEST END ARCHITECTURAL
SALVAGE AND ANTIQUES**
1408 Locust Street
Des Moines, IA 50312
641-751-2937

500 East Locust Street,
Des Moines, IA 50309
515-280-1559

INDEX

Index note: page references in *italics* indicate a photograph; page references in **bold** indicate a drawing.

A

Antlers, *165, 168, 169, 180,* 181
Architectural hardware, *130*
Architectural salvage pieces:
    in living rooms, 97, *97,* 100, *100, 101,* 109, *109,* 115, *115*
    in sunporches/sunrooms, *8,* 9, *9,* 17, *17*
Art, displaying, 35, *35,* 44, *44, 45*

B

Baguette-baker window blinds, *156,* 157, *157, 158, 158, 159*
Ballet bar, 133, *133, 139,* 141, *141*
Barn board, as bathroom wall coverings, *176, 177, 180,* 181
Barn door roller, 111, *111*
Bar/party area, pocket-size, 54, *54, 55,* 56, *56, 57*
Baskets:
    metal, *80, 82,* 92, *92, 176, 177, 179*
    for toy storage, 20, *21, 21, 187, 187*
Bathrooms:
    antique furniture storage in, *172, 173*
    birch tree bath caddy in, *164, 165, 167*
    colors and textures for, *175, 175*
    elegant soap dishes for, *176, 177, 178, 182, 182*
    lights/lighting in, *177, 177*
    old-world reproduction faucets for, *166,* 167
    rustic makeover of, 160–83
    shutter towel shelf in, *164, 165, 168, 168, 201, 201*
    spa features in, *128,* 129, *129,* 130, *130, 131, 132, 132, 133, 133*
    storage in, *128, 131, 132, 172, 173*
    using glass blocks in, *130, 131,* 132
Bedrooms:
    ballet bar in, 133, *133, 139,* 141, *141*
    colors and textures for, *126, 127, 127*
    creative desktop space in, *134, 135, 135, 136, 136, 137,* 138, *138, 139, 140, 140*
    junkmarket style makeover of, 116–41
    makeup vanity in, *124, 125, 125*
    as serene slumber room, *120, 121, 121*
    storage in, *122,* 123, *123, 124*
Bi-fold doors, dressing up, *76, 77*
Birdcage light fixture, *18, 19, 19*
Bongos, as storage, *173*
Bookshelves, *98, 101, 104, 136*
Boot form lamp, 138, *138, 139*
Boot form tray, 87, *87, 89, 193, 193*
Boot racks, in mudrooms, *78,* 80, *80, 82,* 83, *83, 90, 91, 91*
Bottle cap embellishments, *162, 162, 182, 183*
Butler station, junkmarket style, *106, 107, 107*

C

Camp toast votive, 200, *200*
Candles:
    decorating with art paper bands, *119, 121*

holders for, *49, 50,* 51, *51,* 52, *52, 167, 168,* 200, *200*
Caster easels, *31, 32, 33, 33,* 188, *188*
Ceiling tin, framing mirrors with, *177, 182, 182*
Chairs, découpaging, *170,* 171, *171*
Chicken feeders, repurposing, 26, *27, 27, 68, 68*
Clawfoot tub, in rustic bathroom makeover, *160, 161, 161, 164, 164, 165*
Clocks, *118*
Closets, converting space in, 124, *124, 142, 145, 145, 146*
Coatracks:
    with antique hand drills, *84, 85, 85, 93*
    with faucet handles, *76, 77*
    recycling pieces for, *81, 82*
    using doorknobs, 43, *43*
Coffee corner, 60, *60, 61, 61*
Coffee tables, *98, 99,* 101, *101, 104, 110,* 195, *195*
Concrete rug in living rooms, *110, 111, 114*
Corbels, displaying photographs with, *105, 105, 196, 196*
Corkboards, *140, 158, 159,* 198, *198*
Cottage look, contemporary, 116–41
Crafting areas, *62, 65, 68, 68, 72, 73, 73, 74, 75, 75*
Croquet sets:
    mallets as paper towel dispensers, 35, *35*
    storing mops and brooms in rack, *69*
Crystals, *129, 133, 133*

D

Daybed, *4,* 5
Découpaged prayer chair, *170,* 171, *171*
Desks:
    dressing up, *14, 15, 15, 16,* 16
    repurposing pallet as, *142, 146,* 147, 154, *154*
Dining area:
    building a dining table for, *50,* 51
    coffee corner in, 60, *60, 61, 61*
    colors and textures for, *53, 53*
    junkmarket style makeover of, 46–61
    pedestal sideboard table for, 48, *48*
    placecard holders for, *50, 51, 51*
    pocket-sized bar in, 54, *54, 55,* 56, *56, 57*
    seating/chairs for, *46,* 48, *50,* 52, *191, 191*
    window coverings for, *58,* 59, *59, 60, 61, 61*
Dishes, storing, 24, *24, 25*
Dog kennel door, repurposing, *130, 131*
Doorknobs:
    as embellishment, *133, 133*
    making coatracks with, 43, *43*
Doors:
    as countertop, *124, 125*
    as dining tables, *50, 51*
Drawer pulls, *11, 18, 19, 19, 115, 115*
Dressers, repurposing, *104, 105, 105*
Dress forms, *135, 139, 140*

E

Easels for menus/signs, *32, 33, 33,* 188, *188*

F

Fabrics, using vintage prints, *4, 9, 11*
Faucet handles, coatracks with, *77*
Fireplaces, junkmarket style makeover of, *96, 97, 110, 111, 111,* 112, *122, 123*
First aid kit, *90, 91, 91*
Fish stringers, displaying photographs with, *173*
Floors/flooring:
    bamboo, *142, 150, 152,* 153
    linoleum, 160, *165,* 170, *172, 177, 183*
    using reclaimed wood, 130, *131*
Flowers/floral arrangements:
    in fireplaces, *110, 113*
    in glass bottles, *174*
    junkmarket style vases/holders for, 10, *10, 39, 39,* 92, *92*
    in mudrooms, *86, 87, 87, 89,* 92, *92*
    softening effects of, *118*
Fuse boxes:
    disguising, 158, *158, 159*
    as pen and paper caddy, 136–37

G

Game pieces, *32, 33, 33,* 54, *54, 56*
Garden fencing, decorating windows with, *16, 17, 27*
Gauges, recycling, *160, 162, 165*
Glass blocks, *130, 131,* 132
Glass bottles:
    flowers/floral arrangements in, *174*
    as home office storage, 154, *154*
    in laundry room, *62, 66, 68, 68, 70, 70*
    as pencil holders, 35, *35, 37, 62, 66, 70, 70*
Glass lamp shade water fountain, *116, 120, 120, 197, 197*

H

Hand drill coatracks, *84, 85, 85, 93*
Hinges:
    connecting picture frames with, *6,* 7
    hanging curtains from, *72, 73, 76*
Home offices:
    business card holders for, *146,* 154, *154*
    chess corner in, *150,* 152, *152, 153,* 153
    colors and textures for, 149, 150, *150, 151*
    credenza storage for, *145, 145,* 147, *147,* 148
    dressing up desks, *14, 15, 15, 16,* 16
    family workspaces in, 142–59
    junkmarket style makeover of, 142–59
    metal soap dispenser storage/caddy in, *145, 146, 154, 155, 199, 199*
    pallet desk in, *142, 146,* 147, 154, *154*
    personal touches and details in, *148,* 149, 154, *154*
Horse bridle, as toilet paper holder, *180, 182, 182*
Hospital gurney, repurposing, 129, *131*

I

Ice cream parlor stools, *22, 23,* 30, *30*
Iron gate coffee table, *104,* 195, *195*
Ironstone, *107, 113*

J

Juice glasses, 37, *37*
Junk, defined, 2
Junker's toolbox, 185, *185*
Junkmarket style, 2–3

K

Key holders, *42, 43, 43,* 92, *92*
Kitchens:
    colors and textures for, 31, *31*
    cooktop hoods in, *26, 27, 27*
    dining/multitasking area in, *22,* 30
    islands/working areas in, *22,* **25,** 36, *36, 37, 37*
    junkmarket style makeover of, 22–45
    mixing textures and materials in, 39
    mudrooms in, *40, 41, 41, 42, 43, 43*
    sideboards in, 30, *30, 32*
    storage in, *25, 26,* 27
    stove/cooking areas of, *26, 27, 27*
    window coverings in, *28, 29, 29*

L

Ladders, repurposing, *120,* 121
Laundry room:
    basket storage in, *66, 67, 67*
    colors and textures for, 64, 70, *70, 71*
    crafting/sewing area in, *62, 65,* 68, *68, 72, 73, 73, 74, 75, 75*
    detergent dispenser in, *62, 66, 70, 70*
    junkmarket style makeover of, 62–77
    repurposing meat drying rack for, *66, 67, 67, 71*
    storage in, *62, 64, 72, 76, 77, 77*
    window dressings for, *72, 73,* 76
Lazy Susan, *32, 33, 35, 35*
Leaded glass twine holder, *74, 75, 75*
Lights/lighting:
    apple press shade for, 92, *92*
    birdcage light fixture, *18, 19, 19*
    boot form lamp for, 138, *138, 139*
    with industrial clip-ons, *120, 121, 121*
    in kitchens, 34, *34, 35, 35*
    pearl and safety pin embellishment of, 133, *133*
    recycling creative lamp bases, *8, 16*
    in rustic bathroom, *177, 177*
    trash-can lampshades, *8, 16,* 17, *17*
Living rooms:
    butler station in, *106, 107, 107*
    colors and textures for, 97, *108, 109, 109*
    concrete rug in, *110, 111,* 114
    disguising television plasma screen in, *110, 111, 111, 112, 113*
    fireplace makeover in, *96, 97, 110, 111, 111, 112, 122, 123*
    junkmarket style makeover of, 94–115
    reading area in, *98, 99, 99*
    storage in, *104, 105, 105*
Locker units, *40, 41, 41*
Lucite handbags, holding flowers with, 10, *10*

M

Magazine holders, *149,* 163
Mail chutes, displaying photographs in, 148, *148*
Makeup/mirror station, in mudrooms, 87, *87, 89,* 193, *193*
Maps, displaying, *110,* 111, *111,* 112, *113*
Meat drying rack, repurposing for laundry room, *66, 67, 67, 71*
Message boards, 24
Metal art frames, 35, *35,* 44, *44, 45*
Metal baskets:
    in junkmarket style mudrooms, *80, 82, 92, 92*
    storing towels in, 176, *177, 179*
Metal grate:
    as accent in home office, *150, 152,* 153, *153*
    boot drying with, *78, 90,* 92
Metal mesh, as accent in home office, *150, 152, 153, 153*
Metal soap dispensers, as office supply caddy, *145, 146,* 154, *155,* 199, *199*
Mop/brooms, storage of, 69
Mudrooms:
    boot racks for, *78, 80, 80, 82, 83, 83, 90, 91, 91*
    coins/loose change holders in, 87, *87*
    colors and textures for, 88, *88*
    in entryways, 78–93
    junkmarket style makeovers of, *40–43,* 78–93
    kid storage options in, *82, 83, 83*
    in kitchens, *40, 41, 41, 42, 43, 43*
    makeup/mirror stations in, 87, *87, 89, 193, 193*
    storage in, *78, 80, 82, 83, 83, 84, 90, 91, 91, 92, 92*

N

Napkin rings, 92, *92*
Natural light, *2, 8, 9,* 35, *35, 137*
Nesting tables, *4,* 12, *12, 13*

O

Oyster stick curtain rod, *102, 103, 103*

P

Pants hanger, displaying art/photographs with, *64, 68, 68*
Pegboard, 123
Pencil holders, 35, *35, 37, 142, 146, 147*
Pet beds, 36, *38*
Photographs:
    building holders for, 17, *17*
    corbel holder for, *105, 105, 196, 196*
    displaying, 6, *7, 166, 167, 167*
    fish stringer display of, *173*
    hanging from repurposed auger, *166, 167, 167*
    mail chute display of, *142, 146,* 148, *148*
    vintage pants hanger holding, *64, 68, 68*
Picture frames:
    attaching vintage hinges to, 6, 7
    as nesting tables, *4,* 12, *12, 13*
Plastic rain gutters, as window covering, *58, 59, 59, 60, 61, 61*

R

Radiator covers, for bar and wine storage, 54, *55, 56, 57*
Radiator screen, dressing up bi-fold doors with, *76, 77*
Rearview mirrors, as drink holders, *152,* 153
Refrigerator magnets, 24, *24,* 35, *35*
Ruler bulletin board, *140, 198, 198*

S

Sanitary cabinets, displaying miniatures in, 147, *147, 149*
School flash cards, *54, 55*
Sewing areas:
    in laundry room, *62, 65,* 68, *68, 72, 73, 73, 74, 75, 75*
    sharing desktop spaces, *134, 135, 139, 140, 140*
    thread holders in, *65, 72, 73, 73, 192, 192*
Sewing cabinet hall table, 44, *189, 189*

Shelving, brackets for, *20, 21, 21, 187, 187*
Shutters:
    repurposing as table, *107, 107*
    as rustic towel shelf, *164, 165,* 168, *168, 201, 201*
Sink pedestals, as base for buffet table, 48, *48*
Snowshoes, repurposing, 164, *165, 167*
Soaking tubs, in rustic makeover, *160,* 161, *161,* 164, *164, 165*
Soap dishes:
    elegant fixtures for, *176, 177, 178, 182, 182*
    as wall sconces, 49, *49*
Stool-top bench, *46,* 48, *50,* 52, *191, 191*
Storage:
    in bathrooms, *128, 131*
    bookshelves, *98, 101, 104, 136*
    in junkmarket style mudrooms, *78, 80, 82, 83, 83, 84, 90, 91, 91, 92, 92*
    in laundry rooms, *62, 64, 72, 76, 77, 77*
    in mudrooms, *40, 41, 41, 42, 43, 43*
    shelving units for, *20, 21, 21, 187, 187*
    for toys, *20, 21, 21, 187, 187*
    using locker units, *40, 41, 41*
String/twine holders, *72, 73, 74, 75, 75*
Sunporches/sunrooms:
    breakfast nooks in, *18,* 19, *19*
    desk area in, *14, 15, 15, 16, 16*
    junkmarket style makeover of, 4–21
    paint colors and textures for, *10, 11, 11*
    storage in, *20, 21, 21, 187, 187*
Swedish crate shelf, *104,* 194, *194*

T

Tables:
    birdbath as base of, *18,* 19, *19*
    from doors, *50,* 51
    iron gate coffee table, *104,* 195, *195*
    with metal pipes and incubator, *152,* 153
    nesting picture frame tables, *4,* 12, *12, 13*
    from restaurant coatrack, *123*
    sewing cabinet hall table, *44,* 189, *189*
    sink pedestal base for buffet table, 48, *48*
    using warehouse light covers, *60, 60, 61, 61*
Tambourines, serving chips in, 52, *52, 54, 56*
Television plasma screens, disguising junkmarket style, *110, 111, 111, 112, 113*
Test tubes, flowers in, 87, *87, 89*
Thread storage, 65, *65, 72, 73, 73, 192, 192*
Towel holders, *24,* 68, *68*
Trinket holders, *124*
Twine/string holder, *72, 73, 74, 75, 75*

V

Vases, dressing up, 115, *115*

W

Wabash fire door, *40, 41,* 42
Wagons, as storage, *20*
Wall sconces, 49, *49,* 112, *112*
Water fountain, 116, *120, 120, 197, 197*
Wheels, kitchen islands/work area on, *22,* 36, *36, 37, 37, 38*
Whisk brooms, as window treatment, 28, *29, 29*
Windows:
    baguette-baker blinds for, *156, 157, 157, 158, 158, 159*
    curtains for laundry room, *72, 73,* 76
    dressing up, 115, *115*
    hanging curtains from hinges, *72, 73,* 76
    oyster stick curtain rod for, *102, 103, 103*
    whisk broom covering for, *28, 29, 29*
Wine, storage options for, 52, *52, 54, 55, 56, 56, 57, 57*
Wooden crate, as wall storage, *90, 91, 194, 194*